Every Day Is
Father's
Day

JANE SHEWMAKER HALE

DAD, THIS BOOK IS FOR YOU!

_____ Date _____

From: _____

I know you're not much on reading.
There's a million other things
you'd rather do.
But, on a cold or rainy day
And you can't go out to play,
Leaf through the pages,
Chuckle, or shed a tear or two.
This gift is my way of saying, "I love you."

2006 Ozark Marketing and Publishing, DBA Skyward Publishing
info@skywardpublishing.com

Library of Congress Cataloging-in-Publication Data

Hale, Jane Shewmaker, 1934-

Every day is Father's Day / Jane Shewmaker Hale.

p. cm.

ISBN-10: 1-881554-51-1 (hardcover)
ISBN-13: 978-1-881554-51-6 (hardcover)

1. Fathers. 2. Fathers--Anecdotes. 3. Father and child. 4. Hale,

Jane Shewmaker, 1934---Family. I. Title.

HQ756.H323 2006

306.874'2--dc22

2006009863

Cover and book design by Angela Donelle Underwood - www.booksindesign.com

Pa, Cliff, Serle, Norma, Blaine, Mamie (holding Gene)

DEDICATION

In memory of my dad, James Blaine Shewmaker

And, for his sister, Aunt Norma, and his brothers, Uncle Serle, Uncle Cliff, and Uncle Gene. And their spouses, Uncle Howard, Aunt Nelle, Aunt Louise, and Aunt Beulah.

Weekends, holidays, and Sunday dinners together with your sister and brother's families on the Shewmaker family farm gave my brother Rex and me wonderful memories to share with their children: Russell, Marjorie, Harold, Perry, Paul, Carol, J.D., Lyndell, David, Donnie, Kathy, and Sherry, Jack, and Mary Lou Shewmaker.

Bottom: Inez Sadler Shewmaker - Mom; James Blaine Shewmaker - Dad
Top: Rex Juan Shewmaker - Brother; Myra Jane Shewmaker Hale - Author

ACKNOWLEDGMENT

Thanks Dad, for being our link to generations of fathers before you bearing the Shewmaker name.

Thanks, to your dad, Issac Newton Shewmaker, whom we called Pa, for teaching us respect, the importance of tilling the land, and raising a family on the farm during hard times.

Thanks, Dad! You were the rootstock of our family of four: my mom, Inez, my brother, Rex, and myself, Jane, and of course, Dad.

Thanks, Dad! For being a father to our spouses, to my husband Bob, and to Rex's wife, Joan.

Thanks, Dad! For passing your name and love along to our children, your grandchildren:

Ricky, Reggie, Mitchell, and Lucas Hale.

Tom, Joey, Sharon, Connie, and Terry Shewmaker.

Thanks Dad! For being Pa Pa and a special buddy to us all.

THE HALES

Rick: Blaine, Nathan, and Zachary

Reggie and Gai: Chase, Cali, and Colby

Mitch and Suzyn: Nicholas, Chayla, and Austin

Lucas: Jacob

THE SHEWMAKERS

Tom and Barbara: Brian, Amy, and Cortney

Joey and Jeni: Jason, Jana, and Jordan

Sharon and Kelly: Taira, Matt, and Chelsey

Terry and Christie: Ryan, Kayla, and Dusty

Connie and Matt: Emily

CONTENTS:

MY FATHER

My Father is one of the most successful men I have ever known.
He didn't finish high school
Never went to college
Was not well-traveled
Or, a wealthy man.
But, he had friends,
A wife, who adored him,
Children, who admired him,
And, he woke up to a new world every day.

*James Blaine
Shewmaker*

He didn't preach,
Never judged, begrudged,
Or fudged on a bet.
The twinkle in his eye
Was an extension of humor.
Handsome, polite, dashing,
Downright charming,
He turned many a lady's head.
But, was a family man through and through.

Look up the word gentleman,
The definition fits my father.
His world was a good cigar,
Silver dollars for talisman,
Pranks to pull, jokes to share,
Politicians to cuss, politics to discuss.
He never asked much from the world
A little sport, a good business deal,
And, to stay healthy, and see his children grown.

As a child, I looked up to Father,
Never doubted his word,
Or questioned his rules.
He was the center of my universe.
Never a cheater, he was funnier, sweeter,
Than any man I ever knew.
Today, his memory sustains me knowing
The life he lived became my lessons, well learned.

James Blaine & Inez Shewmaker

TWINKLE

I always loved this picture of Dad and Mom
during their courting days.
I wished to be a part of the picture
and would often cry,
"Where O where was I?"
They'd say,
"You weren't here, Jane.
You were only a twinkle in your daddy's eye."

FOREWORD

My wish for all fathers would be
to be
the kind of father
they think themselves
to be.

Researching material for *Every Day Is Father's Day* I found people's perspective of fatherhood to be influenced by which side of fatherhood they were referring to, life as the child or life as the parent/father.

I decided to section the book as I had *Every Day Is Mother's Day* using the letters from the word FATHERS for the name of each section.

F ore Fathers .... Fathers and grandfathers.
A lbum A ttic....................... Reminiscing
T he Kids .... Stories relating to children.
H is & Hers. .... Couples
E very Man.......................... Tributes to fathers.
R ich Man, Poor Man........ Mentors
S houlder High .... A Conclusion

All of the writing in this book is the work of the author with the exception of Section V--Every Man, which features tributes to fathers written by family and friends and acknowledged with their name and profession. Thanks to those whose written contributions are published in this book.

A special thanks to Ellen Gray Massey for her help and editing of this book and *Every Day Is Mother's Day* the companion gift book.

I sincerely hope you enjoy your visit with the Shewmaker/ Hale family in the world of grandfathers, fathers, and father influences.

Read on and find out why *Every Day Is Father's Day* is a world where a man's word is his bond and a gentleman's handshake eliminated a lot of paperwork.

And, families had time to enjoy a home-cooked meal together in their homes while discussing activities of the day.

And, Mother's reprimanded their children by saying, "Wait until I tell your father!"

SECTION I
Forefathers

Issac Newton Shewmaker

In Our Time

He, Who Laughs Last

Grandchildren Are a Reward

ISSAC NEWTON SHEWMAKER

Pa says, "My dad told me it takes a man to reach the top of the mountain, but I learned it wasn't reaching the top but the trip up that made the man.

The walnut four poster bed on which I was born sets beside a matching antique dresser which once belonged to my mom and dad. Atop the dresser in a gold frame is the picture of a young man and woman surrounded by children of varying ages. Three of the youngsters are boys, Serle, Cliff, and my dad, baby Blaine, propped upright in a buggy. Gene, the youngest son was yet to be born to the Shewmaker family. The only daughter, Norma, stands close to her mother, Viola Flo, and near baby Blaine. Even at this early age, Norma seems matronly, an extension of her mother destined to inherit women's work as a sister to four brothers. Viola Flo, clad in a long dark dress with a high neckline framing her oval face, clasps the handle of the buggy. Her dark hair is drawn up and away from her face in the style of the day. One can only image the time and effort she spent getting her young family ready for this group picture.

It is hard to envision these children as the grownups who were my aunt and uncles and the parents of my cousins. Serle and Cliff wear big boy suits with shirts and ties like their dad. Identical derby hats rest firmly atop their heads, giving them a little old man look. The infant Blaine dressed in a long baby dress of white stares wishfully at a pair of horses in harness, possibly attached to a wagon not shown in this picture. A faithful hound rests at the foot of the buggy as if guarding his master. Young Gene, the baby yet to be born, would surely have been nuzzled close to the family dog as his home was always graced by a canine pet in later years.

In the background of the picture is what must have been the Issac Newton Shewmaker family's first home, a modest white frame house with a little front porch.

It is even harder to think of the young couple in the picture as my Pa and Mamie. This young man wore his derby hat firmly planted on his head. Issac's youthful countenance bore resemblance to the remembered faces of my uncles and my dad as I was growing up. Was my Pa ever that young?

By the time I met Pa, he'd lost most of his hair. Self conscious of his baldness he wore his felt derby at a jaunty angle atop his head when outside. Manners dictated the hat's removal indoors. He'd brush the remaining thin strands of hair across the front of his forehead, as if by seeing hair in front, his whole head was covered with hair.

As was the custom of the day, Pa wore a jacket, which covered the small pouch of belly extending over his belt. Mamie teased him about his middle age spread and he responded with a playful slap to her behind, reminding her of other places which might be spreading too. Despite their playful jibes, both were prideful of their appearance. Farm work kept them fit as a fiddle and in tune with the world around them.

Pa Shewmaker was a dashing gentleman. Although he was not tall, his ruddy outdoors-man-skin, almost translucent, gave him a masculine look that blended well with the wispy, white stubble of a beard that graced his cheeks. Crinkle lines at the corners of his eyes deepened with each smile as he shared his brand of humor with us. The shine of a gold cap on his front tooth fascinated us grandkids and added an air of affluence to his otherwise country-bred appearance.

We grew to love this man, Issac Newton Shewmaker. He filled a special place in our lives as we grew from youth to adulthood and from middle to old age. He easily earned our respect along the way. As he lived, he blazed a path for us and our children to follow. Pa was a man of vision who studied the ways of the world around him and nationwide. He was a pillar of the community who was respected by his peers. Farming was a way of life for him and his family. Working the soil to earn a living kept Pa humble and created a closeness with his maker which he passed on to his children and their offspring. Pa was the head of the family and will live forever in our hearts, souls, and minds. He introduced us to the generation of Shewmaker's before us with stories that linked the span of time. It became a tradition of the family to preface stories with Pa said.

Because Pa Shewmaker was my daddy Blaine's father, because he married my favorite person, my grandmother Mamie, and because his seed was my family, he earned my respect as a child. When he chose me to be seated on his knee and talked to me as an adult, I respected Pa most, and he became my hero as he shared with me life's lessons and how exciting the world can be when we follow our dreams.

Issac Newton Shewmaker, my Forefather, you are the paragon of our future. My wish for all children would be that each would know the same kind of fulfillment and adventure we shared as we grew up with you, our loving grandparent. I may not have told you, but I hope you knew that I loved you. And I love you even more today as I've discovered the worth of the man who is gone but not forgotten and whose memory will always be cherished.

Jane Hale Shewmaker

IN OUR TIME

Pa says," In our time we didn't have all the things youngsters have nowadays."

We were raised to remember the Sabbath day and keep it holy. Sunday was also the day Pa expected his family to gather on the southwest Missouri farm where he and Mamie had raised their children. The rich farm land with river bottom acreage sprawled in all directions further than the eye could see. But each of Pa's children and grandchildren knew the land intimately via herding up the cows, picking wild berries, fishing the creek, or cooking out on the sand bars that bordered the creek banks. We had climbed into the loft of the huge hay barns to check on nests of eggs or roll out bales of hay to feed the cattle. With parental warning ringing in our ears, we still ventured into the grain bins where one false step could have sent us to a smothering death. So many adventures beckoned, and so many ventures were yet to be enjoyed as the Shewmaker families returned each Sunday to the place of their birth to enjoy the day together.

The Sunday midday meal was served on the large dining room table laden with enough food to feed a threshing crew. Guests were welcome as they had always been in the Shewmaker home. Mamie's meals were legendary feasts. The hours she spent preparing those meals, peeling mounds of potatoes, preparing dough, punching it down, and shaping homemade rolls to rise for baking, rolling out pie dough to be filled with home grown fruits and pie fillings and skimming rich cream from old bossies milk to churn for butter for seasoning vegetables or to lather corn on the cob was taken for granted as was her other chores.

The fact that she sought out a prize hen, rung its neck, scalded it for picking the feathers, portioned it for frying, and served it up golden brown on a platter was the accepted practice. Even though World War II ration stamps made sugar, coffee, and some staples a luxury, most of the food served was raised or grown on Pa's farm.

It was the custom on the farm to return thanks before meals. After that bowls made the rounds. "Be sure to eat everything on your plate. . . the little children in Europe are starving," was a reprimand every kid I knew heard more than once. We often discussed how leaving food on our plate could harm or help the kids in war-torn countries. But not one of us cousins was brave enough to broach the subject with Pa. We'd been taught children were to be seen and not heard. So, smaller portions became the rule for the children's plates, making it easier to consume every bite. This was a blessing in disguise when bowls held broccoli, cauliflower, or a vegetable we hadn't yet learned to appreciate.

While we worked our way toward dessert, we had a choice of listening to grownup conversation or communicating with our cousins via body language. Adult conversation was filled with clichés to emphasis their stories. As kids, we considered it quite a feat to finish a much--used sentence by mouthing the punch line without getting caught.

If Uncle Cliff told a story about a needy friend, Aunt Louise might toss in the phrase, "A friend in need. . . "

We'd fill our mouths with food and look up about the time the speaker got to the middle of the sentence. Chewing with exaggerated motion, Jack would mouth . . . "is a friend indeed."

One of Pa's favorite sayings that fit almost any situation was, "Nothing is certain but . . ."

Chomp, chomp, ". . .death and taxes."

Pa came from a long line of Democrats. We firmly believed we had been born Democrats. To reinforce that feeling, Pa often reminded his guest, "If my dad thought any of this family voted the Republican ticket he'd . . ."

Working his jaws to fit the unspoken words, Rex would mouth, ". . . roll over in his grave."

Weather permitting, we cousins chose outside activities after dinner. Sometimes when we played baseball, Pa, Dad, and Serle, Cliff, Gene, and Howard came out to join us. Then, they stepped into our world.

Pa was a small wiry man who could throw a slow inside curve that made us back off from the plate. Then, he'd finish off with a fast ball down the center. He chewed snuff and kept a wad of it secreted in his jaw where he'd wallow it back and forth while concentrating on the catcher's glove.

Trying to break his concentration, the boys taunted him playfully. He'd grin, rear back and let that ball fly right over the plate. Most of the time they'd strike out, but they never got mad. They'd always come back shaking their head and grinning at each other like they shared some kind of secret.

I asked Perry about it and he said, "Yell something and watch Pa's mouth, real close."

It took a lot of nerve for me to step up to the plate and pound it with my bat. I watched Pa grin and start his windup. He worked the snuff back and forth, back and forth from jaw to jaw.

I yelled, "I'm going to knock this pitch to . . . "

A wide grin spread across Pa's ruddy cheeks as his jaws moved furiously. His mouth silently formed the words as I finished my sentence, ". . . to kingdom come!"

I stood staring at him as the ball flew across the plate. Had I seen what I thought I had seen?

"Strike one!"

I looked toward Perry who nodded with a grin of encouragement.

I stepped up to the plate again, pounded it, and assumed my hitting stance.

Pa watched the exchange between Perry and me. He nodded and winked at me, saying, "I thought you were going to knock that ball to kingdom come."

"I am, Pa. Throw me another one."

I watched his mouth closely. He wallowed the snuff back and forth ballooning his cheeks and then tucked it into the hollow of one cheek for safe keeping. Just as he prepared to let the ball fly, I yelled, "Pa's a Republican!"

Pa's brows furrowed; his eyes narrowed, and he glared at me. He mouthed, "No, he's not!"

The ball flew over the plate.

"Strike two!"

Everyone was watching as I stepped up for the next pitch.

Pa yelled, "Nobody calls me a Republican and gets away with it, Missy. I'm going to strike you out!" He shifted his wad of snuff and wound up. Stretching his arms above his head he brought them down to his chest. Faster than my mind could grasp, his arm followed through and released a spinning sphere which came hurling straight toward me.

Shaking in my sneakers, I swung wild and connected with the ball. It flew high into the air, out, out, and over the right fielder's head. I didn't stop to look. As soon as the ball cracked against the bat, I dropped the baseball bat and ran. Everyone yelled as I rounded the bases and headed for home. My heart pounded furiously with each beat yelling in my ears run, run, run.

Pa moved swiftly toward the plate to help the catcher cover home. As I sailed cross home plate, I heard Pa yell, "I thought sure I had struck you out, Missy, but you hit a home run."

Panting, I hollered, "I guess nothing's sure, Pa, but death . . ."

Pa reared back his head and roared with laughter. Everyone joined in and soon we were pounding each other on the back and shoulders. Sherry hugged me as Mary Lou and Cathy rolled in the grassy outfield with joyous abandon.

And Russell quoted, "Some where in that favored land the sun is shining bright. And somewhere men are laughing. And somewhere children are having fun. And there is joy at the Shewmaker farm cause Jane just made a home run."

"You misquoted the poem, Russell. And it doesn't even rhyme," yelled Bill.

Russell just winked at me and joined in the fun.

Pa might have thought I was too big for my britches that

Sunday, but he smiled along with me that day when it was my turn to strut my stuff. I'm sure he knew one day I'd be the generation to pass along stories of . . . "Now, when I was a kid."

And, just like always . . . chomp, chomp, he was right.

HE, WHO LAUGHS LAST

Pa says, "He who laughs last laughs best."

The smell of cedar tickled our nostrils transferring the out-of-doors inside as Rex and I came bearing presents to add to the growing pile beneath the sprawling Christmas tree gracing Pa's living room. The great room diminished as the branches reached out to claim areas meant for furniture which had vanished overnight. Up, up, climbed the prickly cedar wood adorned with prized ornaments, hand-me-down tidbits, and revered family treasurers each in their relegated station complimenting the beauteous star atop the branch that touched the ceiling.

"Merry Christmas, Pa. You cut down the big tree down by the branch. How'd you ever get it in the house?" Rex asked.

"Santa's elves themselves delivered it last night." Pa's gold tooth sparkled brighter than the garland on the tree as he teased Rex.

"I guess they decorated it, too." Rex grinned.

Pa spied Mamie peeping around the corner just in time. "Nope, your grandma did that. And a fine job she did, too."

Mamie suspected Pa had seen her and knew if he hadn't he might have claimed the decoration as his own. But everyone knew the hours she spent placing each tissue wrapped prize in its accustomed place. Now, she hugged each of us and helped us tuck our gifts under the lower branches of the cedar and then turned to the door to greet Paul, Carol, Jerry, and Lyndell, whose eyes were shining as they caught their first glimpse of the wondrous tree.

While Marjorie, Bill, and Sherry passed out threaded needles and Aunt Beulah helped us position bowls of popcorn, we began to string the last of the decorations for the tree. In the kitchen Aunt Norma, Mom, Aunt Louise, and Mamie were busy buttering the tops of steaming hot rolls and covering the heaped baskets of bread with tea towels as they carried them to the table. The aroma of cinnamon and brown sugar mixed with butter melted over mounds of sweet potatoes wafted into the great room trying our patience to the limit as we awaited the Christmas feast.

While waiting for the women to finish in the kitchen, Uncle Serle teased Baby Cathy about visions of sugar plums dancing in her head. And as Baby Cathy chortled, we could almost envision the truth of his words. Dad, Uncle Cliff, and Uncle Gene entertained by sharing stories and jokes. Some of the best jokes could be read in Capper's Weekly. After Pa read his copy, everyone else fought to see who could read the paper next so they could read the joke section. Then, they would tell the jokes aloud before the rest could read it.

Being one of the smaller children meant I had to wait my turn for pleasures that seemed to abound on the farm. "You're too little to milk the cow. Stay out of the hen house the rooster might flog you. Don't climb in the barn loft or you might slip and fall. You aren't tall enough to put the star on the top of the Christmas tree. And, you're too little to get to read the jokes in Pa's paper first."

The fragrance of turkey and dressing, gravy and potatoes competed with hot bread and pumpkin pie and Mamie didn't have to call us twice when the meal was ready. Finally the family gathered around the dining room table to enjoy the holiday feast.

"Ker-choo!" The sneeze had hardly escaped before my nose started running.

"Jane," Mom diagnosed my case, "Get your kerchief. You're coming down with a cold. Your cheeks are flushed. Perhaps you should go lie down."

Dad said, "She's just excited. Let her eat with the family. She'll be all right. We'll be opening gifts soon."

Pa nodded and placed the latest edition of the *Capper's*

Weekly on his desk and took his seat at the head of the table. Uncle Howard was the designated Uncle to say Grace. Sometimes he graced the table at length and if we happen to open our eyes to peek, we might see others eyeing the bowls of bounty on the table. Then it was a race to see who could get their eyes closed and head down the quickest.

Today I didn't dare raise my head or lower it quickly because my nose was dripping. "Ker-choo!"

"Jane!"

The food quickly disappeared. "Let's open the presents!" Pa said. Oh! The bounty unwrapped in Pa's living room.

Rex yelled. "A sled. Just what I wanted. Can we go try the snow on the big hill?"

Jack, Paul, Perry, and Rex raced for coats, caps, scarfs.

"Ker-choo!" I wiped my chafed nose and grabbed my coat.

"Jane, you are not going outside. Come, lie on the couch. You can see the hill from the window."

No amount of pleading would change Mom's mind. I sneezed my way to the couch while my cousins trooped out to the big hill to try my brother's new sled.

The grownups helped clear the litter of wrapping paper and settled in by the warmth of the fireplace to talk. I propped myself up on the couch where I could see the hill. It seemed everyone was having fun but me. A big, fat, tear slid down my cheek.

"Ker-choo!"

I felt a comforting hand on my shoulder. A warm fluffy cover was spread over my legs. A paper rustled and settled on my lap. I looked down to see Pa's *Capper's Weekly* lying on top of Mamie's afghan. The newspaper was spread open to the joke section.

Pa's gold tooth shone like a welcome beacon on the stormy sea of tears that blurred my vision. He turned his lips into a downward grimace before positioning his fingers at the corners of his mouth and raising his lips into a smile. He stroked his silky whiskers and motioned for me to read the joke page.

I noticed the paper was not crumpled as it was when Pa finished reading it. I started to protest knowing no one read Pa's newspaper until he finished with it. He placed a finger aside of his nose, slowly shook his head, and handed me a piece of his treasured hard rock candy. He leaned closer and whispered, "Suck on this while you read the jokes. It'll make your throat feel better so you can share the jokes with the old folks."

Laughter filled every nook and cranny of Pa's great room, and I basked in the applause led by Uncle Gene as the grown ups cheered me on with my Christmas debut of joke telling. Just as another hilarious outcry rang out, the door opened and Paul, Perry, Lendell, Jack, Rex and the rest of the cousins trooped in, wet, cold, and bedraggle. I had just read the last of the joke section to the grownups.

"How come Jane gets to read Pa's paper before he does?" Rex asked.

Pa smiled and gave me a sign of approval. "It's just an extra Christmas present."

Warmth flooded through my body beginning at the tips of my toes. It raced up my spine and warmed my lips with laughter. I giggled and it was contagious. Soon everyone joined in and the room was filled with the joy of Christmas as surely as if Saint Nick himself had just joined the party.

Pa winked at me, and I realized he was sharing more than a first reading of his newspaper. He had gifted me with a special act of love I'll never forget.

GRANDCHILDREN ARE A REWARD

Pa says, "Grandchildren are God's reward for not killing off your own children."

"Spare the rod and spoil the child" is an old saying passed down from Pa's generation. It's a handy tool for parents to justify punishment.

As a parent, I better understood some of the sayings my dad said he'd learned from Pa and scattered along the way as he tidied up the task of "growing up his children."

"You'll understand when you're older," followed me to college, marriage, and beyond.

"This hurts me more than it does you." That saying was especially hard to believe when my butt was on fire from being the receiving end of a reprimand.

I found myself muttering the same phase as I applied much needed punishment to my children. It was then I realized butt-hurt is no comparison to heart-hurt. And, I knew this phrase would echo through the years as future generations weighed punishment against misdeeds.

"Just say, NO." I heard this phrase when my children were growing up and thought it was unique to that generation until I realized the phrase was not new, but just the phrasing of it was new. The word, 'Don't' seems to precede rules of my generation as evidenced by the following phrases.

- Don't talk with your mouth full.
- Don't forget your manners.
- Don't make me have to remind you of this again.

- Don't talk back.
- Don't make fun of those less fortunate than you.
- Don't cuss, drink, smoke, or even worse.
- Don't ask for a raise in your allowance. You're lucky to even get an allowance.
- Don't forget to do your chores, homework, etc. etc.
- Don't worry your mother.
- Don't get a whooping at school. If you do, you get a harder one at home.
- Don't try to tell me the F on your grade card stands for anything but FAIL. And, since failure is not in this family's vocabulary, don't fail to hand me that strap and drop those pants as you bend over the chair.

As I grew older, don't grew right along with me.

- Don't think about dating until you're older.
- Don't run with the wrong crowd.
- Don't ask for the family car and don't expect to get a car of your own if you don't help earn money to buy one.
- Don't stay out past curfew.
- Don't get in trouble. If you do, don't let me find out about it from someone else. YOU TELL ME, FIRST!
- Don't do anything I wouldn't do. If you do, don't forget to be careful.
- Don't tell me about the facts of life. I was supposed to explain those facts to you, but since you mentioned it, what did you say about . . . .
- SON, don't ever write a girl's name on a public bathroom wall, and MISSY, don't ever let me find out someone wrote your name on a public bathroomwall.

The don't word followed me through marriage and trickled into my children's lives. I guess the word don't will always be used as long as generations of families are taught to keep on saying NO.

My dad passed along Pa's advice. "If you do your best to try to give your children the benefit of your wisdom, and they refuse to listen, don't be hard on yourself. The good book says God's reward for not killing off your own children is grandchildren."

I didn't ask for chapter and verse on that quote. I said, "Don't worry, daddy. I won't cheat you out of your reward. You can keep the kids anytime."

Dad replied, "There's only one way I'll collect that reward." He reached for his bottle of aspirin and read the instructions out loud. "Take two aspirin AND keep away from children."

SECTION II
Attic Album

This section is dedicated to my cousin Russell who was always a great story teller. In the latter years of his life, he committed many of his stories to hard copy and saved them on CD to share with family. Without his notes, this section would not have been possible.

As the author, I took the liberty of characterizing these stories to fit the attic scenes, but the essence of the stories belong to the Shewmaker family and the attic where we spent so many happy hours on the Issac Newton Shewmaker farm.

A ttic Album

Emotions once touched,
Remember what might
never have been.

Pictures in Albums
Stories from the past
Link generations
Create bonds that last.

SNEAKING IN

Snuggled beneath the eaves of my grandpa's farmhouse was a connection with the past. In the attic were three small rooms jam-packed with remnants from my dad Blaine and his three brothers Serle, Cliff, and Gene's growing up years. Aunt Norma's aura was evident, not from having spent her days and nights in that space, but by an older sister's careful preservation of relics tucked away in small closets, stacked on shelves, and stashed in steamer trunks. Picture albums documenting the Issac Newton Shewmaker family history were a treasure house of memories waiting to be discovered by the next generation.

We cousins retreated to the attic on Sunday afternoons when our families gathered at Pa's farm in Southwest Missouri. Here we were free to play if we abided by the rules of the house. Take nothing, destroy nothing, ask but don't always expect an answer, handle with love, and always leave the rooms tidy. As we prowled the attic, the individual personalities of each of Pa and Mamie's children became more real to us.

A steep stairway near Pa and Mamie's bedroom spiraled upward to the attic. After climbing the first four steps, we had to move back a step to open the door, a tricky maneuver especially if cousins followed close in on our heels. The stairway curved immediately after going through the door. Eight more steps brought the upstairs floor. The last cousin up the stairs was responsible for closing the door. Then we were secluded with the only evidence of our play being footfalls on the wooden floors.

If one of the younger children ran or jumped off a bed

causing family members from below to holler up a reprimand, it was time for a hand-me-down story.

Cousin Russell, Aunt Norma's oldest son, was a born story teller. Because of the difference in our ages, his childhood days were gone before mine began. But as in all families, the stories we heard became the lives we lived and is how this section is documented.

Russell plumped down on one of the iron bedsteads. A multitude of cousins Marjorie, Carol, Donnie B., Jerry, Bill, Rex, Jack, Lennie, Sherry, Paul, and I would pile on the bed beside Russell until the wooden slates, positioned under coiled bed springs, would groan beneath our weight.

"Off!" Russell would order. "Some of you set on the floor." Reluctantly, the last ones to crawl on would give up the delicious softness of the homemade featherbed with its stripe ticking. We clustered on Mamie's homemade rag rug that covered Pa's plank floors and were ready to hear the story.

Russell began, "When Uncle Serle, Cliff, Blaine, and Gene, used to claim these rooms as their bedrooms, they never wanted Mamie to rearrange their furniture.

"Why not?" Donnie B. asked.

"If you want to hear the story, you'll have to be still and listen," Russell said to his youngest brother.

We knew Russell meant it, so we snuggled close to listen.

"The boys used kerosene lamps for light. If they went to bed late at night, they never lit the lamps. They knew how many steps it took to reach their bed and other areas in their room."

"You mean like after we close the stairway door and we know there's eight more stairs to the top?" Donnie B. asked.

Russell frowned at his brother.

"Shhhh!" We all admonished.

"Okay, okay–" Donnie B. groaned.

"Uncle Gene's bed was on a direct line from the staircase, so he'd climb the eight stairs," Russell said, grinning at Donnie B. and nodding. "He'd take three running steps and jump into the middle of his bed. Now Gene had been warned not to jump in the bed because he'd broken several wooden slates which held the bed springs up. When the bed springs fell, the feather mattress collapsed, and the person jumping on the bed fell through the frame onto the floor."

Russell waited until the giggles and laughter subsided.

"When the boys got older, they liked to go into town. Pa set a curfew. If they stayed out past their curfew, they would tiptoe in the dark to avoid waking Pa and Mamie."

"I bet they got caught!" Donnie B. clamped a hand over his mouth realizing he'd spoken aloud.

Russell placed a finger over pursed lips signaling for silence. "Gene had learned to walk easy on the stairs to avoid the squeaky spots. When he eased his way to the top step, he'd take his three running steps and jump for his bed. In this way he avoided getting caught."

"Uh–" Donnie B. began.

We all turned to glare at Donnie B. He looked so abashed we broke into laughter, breaking into Russell's story.

Russell smiled, waiting for the laughter to subside.

"One day Mamie did her spring cleaning and rearranged the rooms, completely moving the beds, dressers, and chests. Pa stayed awake that night determined to catch Gene when he came home."

Russell looked around the group sternly daring anyone to speak and then he continued.

"Gene came in especially late that night."

"I bet he went to see Aunt Beulah." Donnie B. slapped a hand over his run-away mouth. But we all nodded cause we had the same thought. Aunt Beulah and Uncle Gene didn't have any children so they spoiled all of us.

"Where ever Uncle Gene had been, he'd stayed late enough that Pa was already asleep. Gene tiptoed up the stairs, opened the door, eased it closed behind him, crept up the last few stairs and was almost home free. As he gave a running jump to land in his bed, he suddenly remembered Mamie had changed the furniture that day."

We could no longer contain our enthusiasm.

"Oh, no!" Carol cried.

"Poor Uncle Gene," Sherry moaned.

"Quiet! Let Russell finish the story," Jack urged.

"Gene couldn't stop himself and slammed into the dresser. It collapsed under his weight and crashed to the floor. Uncle Gene howled with pain.

Pa awoke. Mamie awoke. The whole family awoke. Pa climbed the stairs to Gene's bedroom only to find Gene faking sleep in his newly arranged bed."

"Way to go Uncle Gene!" Perry said.

"Pa wasn't fooled. He pulled the covers back and found Gene still fully clothed. He asked Gene what had caused the racket. Gene said he'd guessed he'd been walking in his sleep."

Russell couldn't help but smile as he waited for the laughter to stop.

"The next day Pa had a talk with Gene out behind the woodshed and cured his sleep walking." Russell paused and chuckled, "At least until the next time Mamie rearranged the furniture."

"Or until Uncle Gene had another date with Aunt Beulah," Sherry said.

"Uncle Gene probably got the idea of sleep walking from Uncle Serle's accident."

Kathy asked, "Was that when Dad really was sleep walking and walked out the upstairs window?"

"Yes. He fell on a wooden play horse that sat under the window. Mom said he was lucky he wasn't killed."

"Poor Dad, and he wasn't even coming in late," Kathy said. Russell grinned, adding, "At least not that night."

We never tired of hearing Russell repeat the tales he'd learned from Aunt Norma and our grandparents. And Russell never tired of telling family stories.

Smile because it happened.
Recall a happy time.
Memories remain secure
Forever in your mind.

HOOVER APPLES

Apples stored in Pa's cellar gave off a pungent tang penetrating upward into the store room off Mamie's kitchen. The baskets of apples stacked near shelves of canned fruits and vegetables signified fall harvest was catering to culinary needs for the Issac Newton Shewmaker family appetites for the winter months.

Apples were a favorite fruit. After they had been peeled, cooked, and canned they would appear for Sunday dinners as pies, apple cobbler, applesauce, or other recipes calling for the fruit.

If we promised to not make a mess, we were allowed to carry Sunday afternoon apple snacks up to the attic. This was a snack which called for a salt shaker to tart up the taste after crunching a bite from the side of a colossal apple.

Upstairs, with fruit and shakers in hand, we searched for treasures which might trigger a hand-me-down story from cousin Russell.

Delving into one of the steamer trunks, J. D. came up with an old newspaper. He read aloud a few lines of a story "Hoover Apples," named for President Hoover who was most blamed for the depression . . .

"What's a Hoover apple?" Mary Lou asked as she bit into her red apple. She chewed on the fruit and then turned the remainder of the apple around and around in her hands as through the answer might be discovered by examining the fruit.

"Uh, it says here 'turnips became commonly referred to as Hoover Apples because . . .'" J. D. paused.

Russell crawled onto the iron bedstead munching on his apple. He patted the patchwork quilt beside him and motioned to Mary Lou to sit beside him. Cousins piled on the bed and thronged on the floor beside the bed, munching their apples, awaiting the story.

Russell began, "Some of you have heard your folks talk about the great depression, haven't you?"

Most of us nodded solemnly knowing Russell didn't like for us to talk when he told a story.

He smiled. "Well, early in the great depression there wasn't much money to be had. A lot of farmers lost their land. Banks failed. People were without jobs. Those who lived on farms became nearly self-sufficient."

"Does that mean they didn't starve cause they lived on their farm?" Mary Lou asked.

"That's right. They butchered their own meat, canned fruit and vegetables and dried fruits. They filled their cellars with fruit." He stopped to hold up the apple he was eating, "like the apples Pa stores for winter in his cellar."

"Is that how Pa knows to fill his cellar with fruit? Did he and Mamie go through the depression?" Mary Lou said.

"Yes. To hear Pa and Dad tell it the depression isn't over. I have a feeling we'll hear about hard times for years to come," Bill said.

"I've heard Pa talk about farming making him self-sufficient. He has his grain milled for flour, corn meal and animal feed. Mamie makes sauerkraut, hominy, pickles, jellies, and jams," Russell continued.

"He's got the cattle for beef and the cows for milk, cream, and butter. Mamie raises chickens for their eggs. She butchers the roosters for Sunday fryers," Rex said.

We all nodded solemnly remembering the time Rex had been sent to catch a rooster for Mamie to cook for Sunday dinner. The only one he could catch was his pet rooster. His pet was sacrificed for the family dinner. When everyone was seated around the table waiting for the platter of golden brown fried chicken to be served, Rex began to cry. When quizzed, Rex told about his pet rooster that was now the meat for dinner. No one wanted chicken that day. Mamie hastily cut up a ham and removed the platter of chicken from the table.

J. D. was flipping through the pages of the newspaper as he listened. "This story tells about people using the barter system. They'd trade farm stuff for shoes, clothes, gas, kerosene, sugar, salt . . ." he stopped to shake salt over his apple, "and things other people needed that they had."

"That's right," Russell said. "Pa said they used their own wood for heating and cooking. Their poultry feed supplement was bought with cotton print bags. Some of those bags were recycled into parts of their clothing."

I jumped up and twirled around so my skirt panels made a circle. "See Mom still makes my dresses from print feed sacks." Mom was an expert seamstress who made most of my dresses. Sherry reached out and patted down one of the panels of my skirt. "It's prettier than clothes in the Sears Roebuck catalog."

"Our folks learned from their folks and those before them to make due with what they have. That's where the story of Hoover Apples comes from." He stopped to take another bite of his apple. Then he held it up and turned it around and around.

"If you've ever had to eat a season of Hoover Apples, you'll know the difference between this," he pointed to his apple, "and, a Hoover apple."

Harold grinned. "Tell them about the summer we had the late drought and hot period."

"The corn crop was really good that year, but we were short on hay and fodder and late garden produce," Russell said.

"And Dad got the idea of planting turnips as an emergency crop," Harold said.

"Not only did Dad get the idea but all of our neighbors, too." Russell continued, "We must have had a half acre of turnips on our farm. It was an ideal time for turnips that fall. We harvested turnips by the truckload. So did the neighboring farms."

Harold chuckled. "Dad had us dig a large pit and line it with straw for storing the turnips for use during the winter months."

Perry said, "Remember how Dad made us dig the turnips out, chop them up, and mix them with hay and other forage we fed the cattle and sheep?

Russell smiled, "It was a tiresome, never ending job. But the cattle loved turnips and did well on them.

Marjorie nudged Carol. "I guess they are forgetting the family ate turnips, too. Remember how mom had us cook them in every conceivable way."

"Turnip, turnip, turnip greens!" Harold, Russell, Bill, Marjorie, and Perry uttered in unison.

Paul chuckled. "Remember how Dad had us take turns returning thanks before our meals? And when it was my turn I thanked the Lord for everything on the table including the Hoover Apples?" Harold, Russell, and Bill chortled.

"And we all groaned," Russell said. "Pa cleared his throat. In that way he got our attention. And, we made our groans sound like Amen."

"I wonder if that's why I hate turnips?" asked Paul.

"Yep, we all do. You'll never see a turnip on our table again," Bill said.

"Unless Hoover runs for President again," Perry added with a chuckle.

"Pa said the one bright spot of the Hoover Apple period was they didn't have to cut much wood that year," Harold said.

"Yep, he said it was a good year for corn but there wasn't any market for it. Since it couldn't be sold, the only way to make any money from corn was to feed it to the cattle and hogs and sell them," Russell said.

"The price for fattened animals was so depressed that if labor and grain was considered, it was almost a losing proposition," Harold said.

"They used the excess corn as a substitute for firewood. Pa said the bright spot was they didn't have to cut, saw or split much wood that year except for kindling."

J. D. folded the newspaper and put it back in the steamer trunk. We gathered up our apple cores and salt shakers, patted the quilt into place on the feather bed and began trooping downstairs to join the grownups. Jack lingered behind.

40

Sherry called, "You coming down, Jack?"

Jack said, "I'm coming. I was just wondering how many different ways one could market turnips? And if the farmers had too many turnips and found a way to wall them up for major city market. . .well, no telling how many outlets they could build."

"Jack, quit daydreaming. There's no future in it," Sherry said.

As Jack followed the cousins downstairs, the attic settled back to silence and waited for another Sunday, another story, and more memories to share with the next generation who would marvel at the life history of this branch of the family tree.

> *Don't cry because it's over,*
> *Celebrate what you had.*
> *Each time you recall it,*
> *Let your heart be glad.*

LOVE LETTERS

"Did you tell your mom we found her love letters in your dad's old trunk in Pa's attic last Sunday?" Sherry whispered.

"Shhh!" The fact that I was shushing Sherry should have told the answer to her question.

"Sherry, you and Jane know it isn't polite to whisper, especially at the dinner table," Aunt Louise reprimanded.

Sherry mouthed, "Later!"

I nodded and bowed my head while Uncle Howard returned thanks. I was thankful Mom hadn't heard Sherry.

After dinner Sherry and I helped our girl cousins and Aunts clear the table and dry Mamie's dishes. When everything was clean, stored, and the floor was swept, we were free to join the boys upstairs in the attic.

Rex was sitting on the feather bed beside Russell. They had a picture album open between them. As Sherry, Mary Lou, Marjorie, Carol, Kathy, and I came into sight, they looked up and motioned us to come over and see the album.

"Here's a picture of the whole family," Russell said, pointing to a young man and woman. A young girl was standing by the woman holding the hand of a small boy. Two other little boys stood near by. Luggage was stacked in a neat pile by the man.

Rex pointed to each figure as he identified them. "Here's Pa and Mamie," he said pointing to the young man and woman.

Russell placed his finger on the young girl holding the little boy's hand. "That's mom holding Blaine's hand."

Marjorie pointed to the tallest boy. "That has to be Uncle Serle."

Kathy leaned closer to get a better look at her dad.

Sherry moved closer. "Here's Dad."

"Where's Uncle Gene?" I asked.

"He wasn't there. He was just on the road somewhere," said Russell. He chuckled as he delivered the stock phrase meaning someone wasn't born yet.

I giggled. "It looks like they're going somewhere."

Russell cleared his throat. It was his signal he was about to begin a story so everyone hurried over to scoot in close. "Mom said they used to take the train to Kansas City."

"The whole family?" Rex asked.

"Yes. She said it was quite a journey, especially with the little boys because the train trip was long and tiring." Russell pointed to the luggage in the picture. "See the baskets? "We all strained to see where he pointed.

"That's where mom said they packed their food," Marjorie said.

"Didn't they have food on the train?" Sherry asked.

"In those times," Russell said, "everyone brought their own food. Remember times were hard, and they were lucky to be able to travel, especially with their family."

"Isn't Daddy cute?" I leaned closer to get a better look at the little boy holding Aunt Norma's hand.

"Mom said he was as mischievous as he was cute," Marjorie said with a smile.

"What did he do?" asked Rex.

"Cliff and Serle were older and knew they had to sit still, but Blaine was small enough to get away with running up and down the aisles. Mom was sent to fetch him. Sometimes when they napped, he'd get up and roam the aisle again," Russell said.

Marjorie giggled. "Mom said her mother had packed plenty of food, but Blaine found if he stopped to stare at people while they were eating, they would hand him a tasty tidbit, pat him on the head, and send him away."

"Did he eat all the food?" Rex asked.

"No, he'd run back up the aisle and give it to his brothers. Then he'd take off to go and beg some more," Marjorie said. "He had great fun and Cliff and Serle enjoyed the treats until Mamie found out what Blaine was doing. She scolded Blaine for begging and the other boys for nagging him on."

"So, did he quit?" I asked.

"Blaine found a more exciting game. If a passenger was lucky enough to have a seat to himself, the lucky person could stretch out on the hard, board seat, put a pillow under his head and catch a few winks. Blaine found it a great way to pass the time by running up and down the isles yanking pillows from under sleeping heads as he went," Marjorie said grinning.

"Thump, thump, went the passenger's heads as the pillows were yanked out and their head hit the hard, board seat." Russell chuckled.

"What did Mamie do?" I asked.

Marjorie laughed. "Mom said the thumps were loud but not half as loud as the thumps Mamie promised to give Blaine when they reached home."

Paul had stretched out on the floor with his head against a feather pillow and was laughing along with the rest of us. Suddenly Donnie B. reached and yanked the pillow from beneath his brother's head. Paul's head thumped against the board floor.

"Did it sound like that?" Donnie B. asked as he jumped up to run.

Paul was up and after him as Donnie B. headed for the stairs to run to his mother for protection.

"I guess Mom named Donnie B. appropriately when she named him after his uncle Blaine," Marjorie said.

We had all heard the story of how my mom attended Aunt Norma when she had her last child. Aunt Norma had delivered ten children beginning with Russell in 1920. Others followed: Marjorie, 1921, Harold, 1923, Bill, 1926, Perry, 1930, Paul, 1933, Carol, 1935, David, 1938, Jerry, 1940, and Lyndell, 1942. Norma told mom she had run out of names. Mom suggested she name this little boy Donald Blaine after Norma's brother and Mom's husband, Blaine. Norma liked the name and decided to use it for her eleventh child. Mom's only brother was named Don, also, but the baby's name was soon shortened to Donnie B.

When Paul disappeared down the stairs chasing Donnie B., we returned to finding family treasures of the past.

Sherry and I headed for the small trunk that belonged to my dad Blaine. We lifted out a package of letters tied in a blue ribbon. Carefully we pulled one from a stack.

"It's postmarked Oklahoma." Sherry pointed to the front of the envelope.

"What's that?" Rex asked, pulling the envelope from Sherry's hand. He pulled a lined piece of folded paper from the envelope and began to read. "My man. . .I miss you."

Russell pulled the paper from Rex's hand, refolded it, and placed it back in the envelope. He handed it to Sherry and motioned for her to replace it in Dad's trunk. "Those are private letters written to Blaine by Inez when they were courting. If you don't want to get into trouble, you better leave them where Blaine stored them."

Sherry returned the letter to the stack and placed the stack back in the trunk. "Why are the letters postmarked Oklahoma?"

"Mom was born in Oklahoma," Rex said. "She came to visit her cousins who lived near Pa's farm at the Shell Pipeline Station and met dad."

Russell nodded. "My mom said that was the summer of 1929. She remembers Aunt Inez walking with her cousin down to Pa's farm to buy milk. She met Uncle Blaine and he began courting her. When she returned to Oklahoma, Mom said they exchanged letters." Russell nodded to the trunk. "Those must be the letters."

Marjorie smiled. "Mom said the next year Blaine drove to Oklahoma where he and Aunt Inez were married and he brought his bride back to live with his folks here on the farm."

"My man," I said. "That's what mom called dad in the letters. That's so beautiful."

"Oh, that's so beautiful," the boys crooned.

"You boys stop it. If Jane's mom finds out you and Sherry

were snooping in her letters, she'll probably get her butt tanned," Marjorie said.

Sherry and I exchanged looks. We knew Marjorie was right.

"Isn't it strange that the ornery little boy named Blaine grew up to fall in love with Aunt Inez and bring her from Oklahoma to Missouri to live," Sherry said hoping to change the subject.

"Yes, and look what happened then." Russell pointed to me and Rex.

We all thought Russell had made a good joke and laughed about it as we straighten the mess we'd made in the attic. Then we filed down stairs to see what happened to Paul and Donnie B.

"Did you have a good time, girls?" Mom asked.

"Yes, mom. We looked at an album with pictures of Dad in it." I turned to Dad and asked, "Dad, did you really beg treats from passengers on the train when you were little?"

Dad shook his head trying not to smile. "Not that I can remember."

"Did you pull pillows from under passengers head while they were sleeping?" Rex asked.

"Who's been telling tales on me?" Dad looked toward his sister Norma.

"You were a mean little kid," Norma said teasing her brother.

"But he grew up to be my handsome dad, didn't he, mom? Russell told us how Daddy went to Oklahoma and married you and brought you back to Missouri and had me and Rex." I hugged dad.

"It sounds like you got quite an education up in the attic today," Dad said.

"Yes, my man, we did." I clasp my hand over my runaway mouth.

Sherry gasped in unison with the other cousins.

Mom stood, took me by the hand, and said, "Myra Jane, come with me. It sounds like you did more than listen while you were in the attic."

When mom called me by my first name, I knew she meant

business. As I passed Marjorie, she gave me a sorrowful look, and I remembered her prophesy, "If Jane's mom finds out you and Sherry were snooping in her letters, she'll probably get her butt tanned.

And Marjorie was right.

> Sadness makes you gloomy.
> when magic days are past
> Hug tight those moments
> Pictures from the past.

SNIPE HUNTING

School was out for the summer. May was rushing toward Memorial Day. Summer meant playing outside at Pa's when we all gathered for Sunday dinner. Climbing in the hay lofts where we played hide and seek with our cousins or swimming and fishing down at the creek that ran through the bottom of Pa's farm were events we looked forward to after a long, cold winter of being indoors.

We were disappointed when the thunder storm rumbled in during our Sunday family dinner. White hot streaks of lightening snaked along the window panes causing Aunt Nelle to shudder each time the brilliance filled the room.

"We should probably be leaving early, Serle. It may take us longer to drive to Richland in this storm," Aunt Nelle said. Uncle Serle's family lived in Richland where he worked for the Shell Pipe Line. His family had traveled all over the United States and even lived abroad.

"It'll pass over soon. This is nothing compared to the storms we weathered when we worked in the wheat fields in Kansas, is it Cliff?" Serle asked.

"That's right," Cliff agreed. "This storm reminds me of the one that come up so fast the night we took Charlie snipe hunting . . . remember that?"

Serle smiled his wry smile. "Who could forget?"

"What's snipe hunting?" Sherry asked.

"Don't get your father started, Sherry Jean. We'll never get

48

the meal over," Aunt Louise warned.

After the noon meal, we'd been planning on playing ball outside, but the rain kept pouring down. The grownups settled in to visit. The cousins wandered upstairs to the attic.

"Did Dad ever take you Snipe hunting?" Sherry asked her brother Jack.

Jack looked at Rex and winked. "Sure, lots of times. I got me a whole bunch of snipes."

"Me and Jack will have to take you snipe hunting some night," Rex said.

"Really?" Sherry could hardly believe her luck. Most of the time the boys couldn't wait to get away from the girls when they went hunting or fishing.

"Snipe isn't anything like bull frogging, is it?" Sherry asked wrinkling up her nose.

Jack grinned. "Dad and I took Sherry bull frogging down at Greasy Creek the other night."

We looked at Sherry who was nodding. "I got to carry the lantern and burlap sacks."

"Hey, you got the most important part—wading along the creek bank with the light. Sherry, if you hadn't of spotted those frogs with the light, we couldn't have slipped off the bank to catch them and sack them. We must have got twelve or fifteen frogs that night," Jack said proudly.

"The worst part was dressing them," Sherry said, shuddering.

"All you had to do was put their little heads on a chopping block and give their head a whack with the hammer," Jack said, grinning. Carol, Mary Lou, and I shrieked.

"We cut the legs off the body and skinned them," Sherry said, giggling demonically.

"Mom breaded them and fried them in deep fat. They tasted like chicken," Jack said.

Sherry was still proud of herself for scaring us. "The worst thing was when Mom fried the frogs, their legs quivered and jerked like they were still alive." We girls shrieked again.

"So, is it?" Sherry asked. The room was silent. Finally Rex said, "Is it what?"

"Is snipe hunting like bull frogging?"

"No, it isn't," Uncle Cliff said from the top of the stairs where he'd appeared unnoticed. He was followed by Uncle Serle.

"Daddy!" Sherry and Mary Lou said to Uncle Cliff.

"Dad!" Kathy echoed to Uncle Serle.

"Come over here and sit for a bit. Me and Serle will tell you about the night we took old Charlie snipe hunting." Cliff claimed Russell's spot for story telling. Serle sat near him and we all gathered around.

"Sherry, don't let your brother and cousin fool you into going snipe hunting or you'll end up holding the bag." Cliff patted his daughter's shoulder affectingly.

"You mean it's a joke?" Sherry asked. Jack, Rex, Russell, and the boys chortled.

"You might ask old Charlie that when you see him sometime," said Cliff winking at her. "Me and Serle used to go coon hunting and Charlie kept bugging us to go. We knew Charlie couldn't keep up. He'd slow us and the dogs down, but he kept on pestering us."

"One day me and Cliff asked Charlie if he'd like to go snipe hunting that night. Charlie said he would but he'd never hunted snipe. He wondered what kind of ammunition he needed... how he should dress and what he should bring to carry his snipe home in," Serle said grinning.

"The moon was right for snipe," Cliff said with a chuckle, "but they are a species that is scarce. Not many people have spotted them, but in our part of the country they grew mean and fierce."

"Cliff told him to dress warm, wear heavy boots, and tote a big gun." Serle shook his head as though remembering, "When Cliff asked me if I thought Charlie could handle being the bagger, I could hardly keep a straight face."

"Serle played up the importance of being the bagger until Charlie practically begged for the job. Then, Serle taught Charlie how to call the snipe to him." Cliff started laughing.

"Who-who-who! Snipeeeeeeeeee!" Serle let out a blood curling yell that almost lifted us from the floor. We heard footstep running up the stairs. "Who-who-who! Snipeeeeeeeee!" Serle called again as Gene and Dad came into sight at the top of the stairs. They stopped dead in their tracks when they saw everyone setting in a circle around the bed listening to Cliff and Serle.

"What's going on?" Gene asked.

"Dad and Uncle Serle are teaching Charlie how to hunt snipe," Sherry said.

Gene and Dad started laughing. They sank to the floor beside us to listen to the rest of the story.

"Charlie was a quick learner," Serle said. "By that evening when we met at the edge of the woods, he had his Who-who-who! Snipeeeeeeeee down pat."

"It was about eighty degrees that night, but Charlie was bundled up like he was dressed for a snow storm. He had his wading boots on and was carrying a burlap bag big enough to put an elephant inside." Cliff shook his head remembering.

"We kept instructing Charlie on how important his job was and how he had to remain alert no matter what happened. And, above all, not to turn on any lights or leave his post once he got to the place on the snipe trail," Serle said.

"Poor old Charlie was so excited he could hardly stand it. This was one of the most important jobs he'd ever been chosen for, and he was determined to do it right. We told him we were going into the wood to flush out the snipe and head them his way. We reminded him to call them at five minute intervals and to be brave when the creature appeared and not to get scared or it might attack him," Cliff said as he laughed.

"Cliff had Charlie do the snipe call again to be sure he had it right. Then, he patted him on the shoulder and told him if he did the call just like that the animal would go right into his bag. Then all he had to do was tie up the top and hit out for the road where we'd meet him and go show off our catch," Serle said.

"After we got out of Charlie's sight, Serle and I took off down the snipe trail. We cut through the woods heading back for our truck," Cliff said.

"Who-who-who! Snipeeeeeeeee," Serle cried and he and Cliff hugged each other while tears ran down their faces.

Gene and Dad were laughing almost as hard. The boy cousins joined in and the girls caught the bug and giggled.

"We sat in the truck for about an hour listening to Charlie hoop out his snipe call as he waited for the creature to descend on him. That's when the thunderstorm blew in and the rain came down. Finally, we started up the truck and went home," Serle said.

"You left Charlie in the woods calling Who-who-who! Snipeeeeeeeee in the storm?" Sherry asked.

"Yep. We didn't want to scare the snipe away." Cliff chuckled.

"Funny thing, though. We saw him the next week and he didn't mention a word about snipe hunting," said Serle grinning.

"Never bothered us to go coon hunting again, either," Cliff said.

"In fact, if he ever acted like he wanted to make a nuisance of himself, all we had to do was call Who-who-who! Snipeeeeeeeee and old Charlie took off faster than he could holler Who-who-who! Snipeeeeeeeee." Cliff hugged Sherry. Then he slapped Serle on the back and they went downstairs chuckling with their brothers.

"So, is it?" Jack asked.

Sherry looked at her brother. "So, is it what?"

"So, is it a good night for you to go snipe hunting and do you think you can learn the call? Who-who-who! Snipeeeeeeeee!" He gave her a playful shove and ran for the stairs.

"Who-who-who!Snipeeeeeeeee!Who-who-who!Snipeeeeeeeee!" We all hollered as we ran down the stairs to join the grownups.

And the attic once more became silent, except for the pitter-patter of raindrops and the flash of neon brilliance spotlighting the windows like a snipe hunter on a dark night in the lonely woods.

SECTION III
The Kids

THE KIDS WORLD

The kids section connects Section II to Section IV like children create ties between a man and woman who become a father and a mother when they create a child together.

Kids are a re-creation and reminder of the growing up years when one's life was shaped by adult/parental guidance. The shaping of those years is an adventure that leads to the land of adulthood, where the product of childhood provides opportunities for the grown child and the parent/influence to create an adult relationship. Each generation adds another branch to the family tree with children unique to their era.

The kid's world is a wonderland of one-way trails with roller coaster ups and downs and stories to share at bedtime.

My brother-in-law once said to me, "I miss my kids."

I replied, "You can visit or call them anytime."

He said, "Oh, I don't mean those adults. I miss the little kids they once were."

So, fathers, enjoy the pulley-bone-make-a-wish-days while your kids are growing up. And, enjoy them second hand as you read the section in this book, The Kids.

54

EVERY DAY IS SUPER DAY AT HOME

Single men don't know what they're missing! Every night when I come home it's like entering a different world.

Yeah! Super World, that's my home!

Our nine-year-old, Superguy, flies through his homework, which has to be completed before he can tune in his counterpart on television.

His younger brothers, Bat Fellow and Sparrow, duel their way through daily chores. Justice reigns in our household.

The one child, untouched by the super craze is little Ginny, Daddy's girl.

She stakes out her daddy's lap, no poachers allowed. Thumb in mouth, she sucks contentedly, while I tell her about my day. Now, that's my idea of Super World!

Tonight, that all changed.

Ginny, seated on my lap, was listening to my day when suddenly she suctioned out her thumb and announced, "I'm S-2, T-2!"

I scooped her up hastily and deposited her carefully by my chair, "Go tell Super Mama," I suggested. "She's in charge of those things."

Ginny stiff-jointed in to Mama chanting, "Over and out! Over and out!"

It hit me like a ton of bricks. Ginny Robot had orbited into Super World.

Super Mama announced refueling time. The Super clan claimed their perches. Bat Fellow and Sparrow beamed in on a star spangled dinner of hamburgers and the works. Superguy downed his formula Z super-class milk.

The new Super-Wonder droned, "Pass the corn, over and out, over and out, over and out!"

Super Mama commanded the forces as she refueled the Mother Ship.

Even Super World has a lights out!

Behind the closed doors of our bedroom is when my world becomes solid reality. But tonight, I finally surrendered my identity to Super World as Super Mama and I wrestled over the electric temperature control on our king-sized blanket.

After enduring all I could of a blanket tug-of-war, I leapt to my feet, swept away the blanket from Super Mama, and flung it around my shoulders like a giant cape. Dramatically, I leered at the mother of my super clan and delivered these lines, "Never fear, Super Mama, I'll keep you warm!"

She squealed in delight, "Oh, you great, big hunk!"

"Hulk, my dear, the unbelievable hulk! And, I'd advise you to not trifle with the Hulk!" With those words, I claimed my title.

She reached over and patted the mattress beside her and gloated, "Welcome to Super World! I knew you'd make it."

And that, my friend, is the way super characters are made!

FAST FOOD

"Hey Dad," I asked my father, "What was your favorite fast food when you were a kid?"

Dad grinned, "No fast food at our house. Mom cooked every day. When Dad and us boys came in from work, we all sat down together at the dining room table to eat what she had prepared."

"You mean you didn't get to order in? What if you didn't like what your mom cooked? Or, weren't hungry for what she fixed that day?"

"That wasn't an option. When we came in from work, we were usually so hungry anything tasted good. Besides, my mom's food was better than any fast food. You've eaten your grandma's cooking. What do you think?"

I nodded, remembering my grandma's table laden down with food. But, her food was meat, potatoes, vegetables, and stuff. How could you eat that every meal? I asked, "What about pizza, tacos, burgers, and fries?"

"Sure I like pizza, but I was almost grown before I tasted my first pizza. Me and my friend had heard of this place that served pizza pie and we decided to take our girl friends there for a treat. His girl friend took a big bite of the pie, burned her mouth, and demanded to leave."

"Did you?"

"Did I what?" Dad asked.

"Leave," I repeated.

"Of course we did-- after we finished every bite of that hot pizza pie.

"But when you were a kid, you ate what was on the table?" I prompted him.

The memory of his first pizza pie faded and Dad nodded his head. "Like I said, you ate what was on the table. If you didn't like it, you sat and watched the others eat until everyone was finished and you could asked to be excused and leave the table." I laughed, trying to imagine eating meals that way. Then, I noticed how Dad was looking at me. I'd seen that look before and knew I was in for a lecture which would start, "When I was growing up . . ."

Sure enough, he motioned to me to be seated at the table and he began, "You kids have it too easy today. When I was growing up, we worked right along side our parents to help put food on the table."

While I sat there listening, my dad reminded me of the difference in the two worlds in which we grew up. "My parents never owned their home, or farm, until I was almost grown.
We wore Levis, but they were the working kind, not the fashion kind." He eyed the fashion holes in my jeans. "If our Levis had holes in them, it was because we earned those holes by doing hard work."

I nodded.

"My Pa never set foot on a golf course." I smiled remembering my dad's opinion of playing golf. If you want to walk all over a field trying to knock a ball in a hole, you might as well be carrying a hoe and cutting thistles on the back forty.

Dad continued, "Pa never traveled out of the country. He didn't have a credit card." He stopped to consider, then said, "Pa did have a charge card he used at Sears and Roebuck."

"Is that the same as Sears at the mall?

"That's what they call it today. Somewhere along the way Roebuck dropped out. We got our first television set at Sears Roebuck when I was almost eleven-years-old."

"You had color television?"

"Nope, black and white," he said smiling, "until Mom bought a piece of plastic that was colored to cover the screen. It divided the screen into thirds and each third was a different color. You can't imagine."

"Er, dad, I've got to go to ball practice. You think we can talk about this on the way?"

Dad motioned me to follow as we started for the car. He continued, "My folks never drove me to ball practice. We didn't practice. We just played. Pa didn't own a car, just an old farm truck. And, it wasn't for taking kids to ball practice."

As Dad started the car, his cell phone rang. He answered it, grunted several replies, and hung up. "The only phone we had when I was growing up was in the kitchen. It hung on the wall and was on the party line. You didn't dial until you listened to be sure no one was on using the line. Then, you hoped they weren't still listening while you made your call."

We had reached the ball park. I started to slip out my door, relieved that I wouldn't have to listen to any more of Dad's tales, when suddenly I remembered I would need some money to get a burger and fries when the coach drove me home.

Reaching my hand toward Dad, I started to ask --

Recognizing the gesture, Dad said, "When I was your age, I earned my own money delivering newspapers six days a week. The paper cost eight cents per paper. I got to keep three cents from each one sold. On the weekend, I collected the money and sometimes I even got a tip." Dad reached into his pocket and pulled out a bill and handed it to me. "Here's you a tip, son."

I looked for extra money, but the tip my dad had for me wasn't money and his words of wisdom didn't make sense until I was much older.

"Don't spend all your money in one place. And, remember, a penny saved is a penny earned." Seeing my puzzled expression, he finished, "You'll understand when you're grown and earning your own way."

A LITTLE KNOWLEDGE

If I were lucky enough to accompany Dad to Dillion's Drug Store, just up the street from his service station, it was a special treat. What he ordered depended on the number of fellows at the store at that time and how long they had to spend talking. A cherry coke meant it would be a short visit. A thick chocolate malt meant sit back, relax, be still, and don't tell Mom what ruined your appetite for the next meal.

Jake, one of the proprietors, could make the best fountain drinks ever. He served them with a chuckle and sometimes a good joke.

While I enjoyed my malt, I listened to the men's conversation. I'd been cautioned about eavesdropping and cursing. As I listened, I learned about both.

Somewhere around 1943, when I was nine, the sports enthusiasts were saying the World Series would one day be played in St. Louis between two St. Louis teams.

One of the men said that had as much chance happening as a Black playing for the Brooklyn Dodgers or Commissioner of baseball, Judge Landis, lifting the ban on the Chicago Eight. Landis would die before he let that happen.

Someone else predicted all those things might happen When hell froze over. That caught my attention. How could hell freeze over?

The conversation switched to politics. Dad was a strong Democrat, an even stronger F.D.R. man.

One of Dad's friends said, "Let me give you a little inside tip, boys. One day we'll see a Missouri Baptist Democrat in the

White House."

That's when the other man repeated, "When hell freezes over."

The gentleman laughed. "That's the best tip you'll ever get boys. Don't forget where you heard it."

Later that year I learned another meaning for the word tip. Mom raised battery chickens. She had a good business selling them after she'd killed, dressed, and delivered them to the neighbors.

My job was to deliver the fryers on my bicycle. One of the neighbors, Mr. Jenkins, had become my friend. We often talked when I made a delivery.

As I started to leave, Mr. Jenkins pressed an envelope in my hand, and said, "I have a tip for you."

My mind instantly returned to Dillion's Drug Store and the conversation about politics. Mr. Jenkins and I had never discussed politics, but, I waited for his tip.

He smiled. "Your mother does a good job with her chickens, and you make a nice delivery girl."

When I got home, Mom checked the envelope, smiled, and handed me a quarter. "Honey, did you know you got a tip?"

My mom knew everything! But, how could she have known about Mr. Jenkin's tip?

Mom looked at me strangely. "Mr. Jenkins did give you a tip, didn't he?"

"Yes, Mom. He said you raised good chickens, and I was a good delivery girl. Some tip."

I turned the shiny quarter over in my hand as Mom gave me another definition for tip--a reward to someone who has provided good service.

By the time I was twelve, I thought I knew everything. Did I have a lot to learn. I still loved to go to Dillion's Drug Store to listen to Dad's friends and watch Jake preside over his fountain as he told jokes. One day I leaned on the marble counter watching Jake dip ice cream from the depths of his back counter. Startled, I saw little wisps of vapor rising from a container.

"Jake, I think something's on fire." I gripped my half dollar tightly, forty cents for the malt, ten cents for a comic.

Jake gave a devilish laugh and raised the lid. Steam hissed. He urged me to look closer.

"What's happening? I see ice, but it's steaming." I waited breathlessly for an answer.

"It's dry ice. Don't ever touch it. It's hotter than heck." Jake closed the container.

My malt, my comic were forgotten. I had found the answer to a question that had bothered me for about three years. "Gosh, it's like hell's frozen over and someone chipped their way out."

Jake roared with laughter. He was still chuckling about hell freezing over as I walked to a booth to drink my malt and ponder my new-found knowledge. I reviewed the conversation I'd heard three years ago.

I realized the St Louis Cardinals had beaten the St Louis Browns for the World Series in 1944.

I'd read Judge Landis ruled baseball strictly until his death in 1944.

In 1947 Jackie Robinson had become the first Black to play in organized baseball for the Brooklyn Dodgers.

Harry S. Truman, our very own Missouri Democratic Baptist, was now President.

And ... hell had frozen over. I had just seen it with my own eyes in Dillion's Drug Store. Everything Dad's friend predicted had come to pass.

Full of malt and answers, I left my dime on the table.

Just as I reached the door, Jake hollered, "Hey, you forgot your dime."

"Keep it Jake. It's a tip. You just provided the best service I ever had." I pushed through the door onto the familiar streets of my hometown to the echo of Jake's laughter. I couldn't wait to get to Dad's service station and tell him what I'd learned.

THE CHRISTMAS TREE

The tree looked small and scraggly surrounded by taller, grander cedar trees on my Pa's farm, but we kept returning to examine it again.

"Take your time. There's plenty of trees. Just remember last year!" Dad's voice carried on the cold air and drifted to where my cousins and their fathers were searching for their Christmas tree. Dad examined each tree we viewed, but he always returned to the little, misshaped tree.

"Oh, Pop, here's my favorite tree," my cousin called."We all turned to look. It was a grand tree. We leaned our heads back and gazed upward. A light spray of snow sprinkled the tree's green branches grazing them with a powered sugar icing like Mamie's Christmas cookies.

"Look. It's perfect!" My cousin danced around the huge tree.

We joined her. Around and around the tree we circled. It had no imperfections. Once more we looked upward. The tree ended in a point outlined against the sky. When dusk captured the woods, one could imagine the evening star gracing the tree top. In branches far above, we spied a nest. Listening, we heard small chirps as baby birds waited for the return of their mother.

Other trees stood naked, shivering, their branches bare. Their time had come and gone as seasons changed. Summer's abundance of green leaves had turned to shades of gold, bronze, and red when Jack Frost visited Pa's farm. The beauty of autumn had been brief. Leaves crackled under foot as we examined the tall cedar. Dried brown leaves wedged among branches of the cedar decorated the tree as nature intended.

Even as we marveled at the beauty of the cedar, we knew it was too large. Dad's reminder of last year's tree was still fresh in our mind.

Last year we persuaded Dad to cut a tree not nearly as large as this one. We helped drag it to the wagon, hoist it on, and proudly claimed it as our Christmas tree. When we got back to Pa's house, we all unloaded our trees. Ours was the largest and the most perfect, but it was too large to transport to our home. Mom reminded us that even if we got it home, we would never have room for it in our small house. Pa came to our rescue and told Dad to cut the top out of the tree.

Glumly, we watched Dad butcher our beautiful tree. When he was finished, he stood a perfectly shaped tree before us. We couldn't believe our eyes. Dad loaded the little tree in the trunk of our car and tied the lid down to hold it.

Pa shook his head sadly. "What a waste." We looked at the remainder of what had been a beautiful tree. Now, it was nothing but bottom branches with no future except to become a home for fish in Pa's creek.

Dad saved the day. "Who needs boughs of holly to deck their halls?" He began sawing limbs for his brothers to take home for greenery.

Pa sighed, "It's a shame to waste God's creations. Some trees are big, some are small, some are made to live in the woods, others to become Christmas trees."

As we stood admiring the big cedar, Pa's words came back to us. We turned and continued searching for trees destined to become Christmas trees. Everyone picked a tree and the men began sawing.

My brother, Rex, and I returned to the small tree with Dad. "We need to make up our mind. It's almost time to go home," Dad said.

Rex and I nodded and Dad pulled out his saw. In no time our tree fell to the ground. Dad grabbed the top and hoisted it to his shoulder, and we made our way to Pa's wagon.

The uncles unloaded their trees as the aunts eyed their selections. Mom nodded her approval at the size of our tree. Then, she walked around it surveying its body. One side was sparse . . .the other side was bare, spindly limbs.

Mom reached out and patted the well-shaped side of the tree. "We'll put the tree in the corner. This side will be nice to decorate. The other side will fit well in the corner. We won't need as many decorations because the back of the tree will never be seen."

Dad picked up our tree and started to load it in the trunk of our car. When Pa nodded his approval, we knew we'd picked the right tree. This tree was meant to be a Christmas tree, our Christmas tree.

LITTLE GIRL DREAMS

My dad used to say, "Even the plainest of women are pretty when they dress up to get married."

Sitting in the pew beside my family, I watched the beginning of the wedding with interest. Men, dressed in what my dad called monkey suits, escorted guests to their appointed side of the church. Then, they seated the mother's of the bride and groom.

The preacher appeared behind the podium. The groom and his friends wearing monkey suits came in to stand to one side of the preacher. Ladies floated down the isle in pastel-colored gowns.

The music became serious--dum, dum, de-dum. Everyone turned to look at the back of the room where the bride and her father stood together poised to walk down the isle. Little girls scattered flower petals along the isle in anticipation of the bride. A ring bearer carrying a pillow to cushion the wedding ring walked stiffly forward.

"Stand up!" Dad nudged me as he and everyone else in the church stood as a compliment to the bride.

The music rose and fell as the bride and her father smiled at each other and began to march down the isle. The moment had arrived! The bride's flowing white dress bellowed around her with each step. The wispy thin veil covering her face gave her a mysterious air. As she walked, her long-flowing dress was supported by two little boys who were jump-stepping, trying to keep up.

66

As the bride came even with our row, I strained to see her face. Luckily, I was able to see her features, and I studied her eyes as she looked straight ahead, focusing on the man who was to become her husband. When the wedding possession reached the front, the bride stood on one side of her father, the groom and his friends stood on the other side.

"Who gives this woman?" the preacher asked.

The bride's father answered, "I do." Then, he looked toward where her mother sat and repeated, "Her mother and I do."

A lump stuck in my throat, my eyes blurred with tears, and pain grabbed my heart and twisted. Tears began to roll down my cheeks, and I moved closer to my Dad's side.

Dad pulled his handkerchief from his pocket and handed it to me. I dabbed at my face blotting tears.

The thought of the bride's parents giving her away to the man who was going to promise to love, honor, and protect her as long as they both should live, filled me with sadness.

Dad leaned down and whispered, "What's the matter? Weddings are supposed to be a happy time."

Holding Dad's handkerchief in one hand, I placed my other hand in his and squeezed. "You won't ever give me away will you?"

"Not unless you ask me to." He smiled down at me. "You think you'll ever do that?"

"I do," I mouthed the words along with the bride.

"I thought so," said Dad smiling.

"No, Dad, I wasn't talking to you. I meant . . ." I hesitated.

"I know. Don't worry about it. It'll be a long time before we walk down that aisle together."

"Till death do us part . . ." The vows were final.

"You may kiss the bride," the preacher told the groom, who lifted his wife's veil and gave her a big kiss right there in front of everyone.

I pushed closer to Dad's side and buried my face against his suit coat. Dad was right. It would be a long time before I became a bride. But, I could dream about the dress, the veil, the flowers and all the things that little girls dream of until that chosen day. I wasn't ready for my daddy to give me away, but wedding frills were enough to fill my dreams for a long time. And, one day…

And one day like all little girls, I grew up, left my dad and mom and pledged my allegiance to the man I'd spend the rest of my life with. Love comes to us all, if we're lucky.

The other day I was asked to write a poem for a couple's wedding. It brought back memories of a little girl's wedding dreams and the days when every day was Father's Day.

A WEDDING PRAYER

I walked alone,
No need to share
Sun on my face,
Wind in my hair.

Content to watch
But not to chance
A broken heart,
Ruined romance.

My world was empty.
What could I do?
You filled the void
When I met you.

Two gather to share
What one might miss.
Love and laughter
Wedded bliss.

Two hearts beat as one
Love enough for three.
Together forever
We become family.

WORRY WART

*"Rails and Snails and puppy dog tails.
That's what little boys are made of."*

"Did you ever have a wart?" Miss Davis waited patiently while second grader hands raised and began to wave.

"Yes, Jane?"

"I guess I've been a wart since I was born."

"Oh, really. What makes you think that?"

"Dad says I've been a worry wart for as long as he can remember."

Some of the class laughed along with our teacher. Others looked around blankly asking, "What's so funny?"

"Jane, I guess you have just proved there are different kinds of warts. Can anyone else think of another kind of wart?"

"My neighbor calls her husband an old wart hog," Jimmy informed Miss Davis.

"Do you know what a wart hog is, Jimmy?" Miss Davis asked.

"I asked my grandpa. He said it was the ugliest animal in the world. He showed me a picture. It had horns--only they were on its nose. It looked like a big hog only it had a mane, and it was gray with thick hide and it lives in Africa," Jimmy said beaming.

"You have a good memory, Jimmy. Did your grandpa tell you anything else about the wart hog?"

He said my neighbor probably called her husband an old wart hog because men wart hogs prefer to be left alone. And, she said he had warts on his-- ."

"Jimmy! I believe you've told us enough."

"Face," Jimmy finished.

Raymond, the boy seated in front of me turned around and placed his hand on my desk. "There, right there!" He pointed a grungy finger at a small seed looking lump on the side of his thumb.

"Raymond! Jane! What are you doing?" Miss Davis walked to our desks.

I looked at Raymond. He, again, pointed to his thumb. I had seen boy's dirty hands before. After all, I had a brother.

"Miss Davis, Raymond just laid his hand on my desk. I don't know--."

Raymond extended his thumb in Miss Davis's direction. She stepped back. "Why Raymond! You have a wart on your thumb. Would you like to come up front and show it to the class?"

Raymond looked around at the class. He wasn't in the habit of being the center of attention. He, certainly, wasn't in the habit of standing in front of the room with an answer. "Er, I was just showing Jane."

They looked at me. "Go on, Raymond. If I had a wart, I'd show it."

Raymond walked toward the front of the classroom as the kids cheered.

Miss Davis followed him. She said, "Class, please quiet down. Raymond, do you know how you got this wart?"

Raymond looked at her as if she'd accused him of stealing. "It's mine! My thumb started itching. Mom told me not to scratch it. One day when my Pa took me fishing he told me it was a wart."

"Raymond, if the class would like to see your wart you could walk around to each desk and show it."

Raymond grinned and started his tour.

"Please class, don't touch it. Warts can be spread from one person to another," Miss Davis warned.

Billy was waving his hand furiously.

"Yes, Billy?" Miss Davis said.

"Does that mean if we wanted a wart we could get one from Raymond?" Billy asked.

"Billy! Warts are only infections if they are scratched open. Raymond's wart is not that way. I repeat, do not touch it!"

While Raymond walked around showing off his wart, Miss Davis continued telling about warts. "As you can see a wart is a horny growth on the skin. They can appear anywhere in a wide range of shapes, sizes and numbers."

Johnny raised his hand.

"Yes, Johnny?"

"My Pa had a wart on the bottom of his foot. He said it looked like a corn but it hurt like he--."

"Johnny!" Miss Davis snapped.

"Heck, I was going to say heck, Miss Davis. Pa said you could get warts anywhere even on your lips or tongue or--."

"Thanks Johnny, anyone else?" Miss Davis asked.

I raised my hand. "Miss Davis, I know animals have warts. My mom told me not to pick up a frog because I could get a wart from him. I picked one up and my hand is itching. Do you think I'm getting a wart?"

"Animals do have warts but an animal can't give a person an animal wart. Tell your mom, contrary to superstition, you can't get a wart from a frog."

"Miss Davis, my finger is still itching. I touched the desk where Raymond had his hand. Do you think I could have got a wart from him?" I asked.

"Jane, your dad was right. You are a worry wart. And, I believe we have spent enough class time on warts. Raymond, if you'll take your seat, it's almost time for recess."

At recess we all got a better look at Raymond's wart. Somehow it got scratched--! You guessed it. . .the second grade had an epidemic of warts that year.

PAPER PLATES

This story, or one like it, may cause you to think twice before relegating a person of age to a lesser station in life.

Great Pa out lived grandma and chose to live alone until his health failed. Then, he came to live with his son, his daughter-in-law, and his small grandson.

The small boy was Great Pa's shadow and mimicked his every move. The boy's sure steps soon became shuffles as he followed in his Pa's footsteps. His table manners suffered when his hands trembled in sympathy with his elders. After numerous spills, broken plates, glasses, and wasted food, the son and daughter-in-law put a table in the kitchen for Great Pa and tried to recover the ground they'd lost with their son.

Great Pa ate alone in the kitchen while the family enjoyed their meal in the dining room. When Great Pa's table habits became worse and he broke dishes, he was served his meal on a paper plate. When the grandson went to the kitchen to get a glass of water, he noticed Great Pa had tears in his eyes as he sat alone eating his meal from his paper plate. The boy hastened to pick up food on the floor and refilled his Pa's overturned glass, wiping up the remainder of the mess he'd made before he returned to the dining room to finish his meal in silence.

One day the young boy's day care teacher sent home a picture the boy had drawn. His parents admired their son's drawing of a house. On the outside were written the words, My House. Inside the house were two people sitting at a table eating a meal. Beside the table was a stack of round objects almost as tall as the table. In another room was one person sitting at a table eating by himself.

His father asked, "Who are the people in the picture?"

The boy pointed to the person eating alone, "That's me, eating in the dining room."

The father asked, "And, who are these two people?"

The boy replied, "That's you and mom eating your dinner in the kitchen."

"Why are we eating in the kitchen?"

"Because I'm grown up and you're old," the boy said.

"And, what is this stack beside the table?" asked the father.

"That's your paper plates," the boy said.

That very night Great Pa was invited to join the family in the dining room for his meal. The parents didn't seem to notice when he dropped his napkin, spilled his milk, or missed his mouth with food.

But the young boy noticed and helped his Pa with his food smiling all the while. Soon, everyone was helping Great Pa and mealtime became a happier time for the family. For the rest of his life Great Pa ate with the family in the dining room.

SECTION IV
H is & Hers

COMPLETE SERENITY

You know what I miss?
Yeah, that, too!
But I really miss - you.
Long talks,
intimate walks
evening fading into
dawn,
and, we've not even gone
to sleep.
Business discussions
forming plans,
partnering, holding hands,
relating stories a lifetime ago.
Our world resides in
long cozy rides
sandwiched
between slices of time.
When we leave the world behind
and, you're completely mine.

You know what I miss?
Complete Serenity - you!

DEARLY BELOVED

Once upon a time romance was a bowl of cherries served up for public eyes to view as a scrumptious dessert. Courtship blossomed, romance flourished, and couples said their vows before dewy-eyed young maidens and gentlemen, who fidgeted in tux and tails. The days of honeymoons abroad, engraved initial silver, linens, and matching bathrobes, wound a gossamer web of enchantment over the scared union of matrimony and fluffy bath-towels proclaiming His & Hers.

Love still thrives and romance leads to wedded bliss but, too often, now-a-days, the gild of innocence adding serenity to the joining of "this man and this woman" has been replaced with "let's get this show on the road" because there's nothing new under the sun to bring to the alter.

The days of courtly gentleman and demure young maidens, for the most, has been replaced by unimaginative monograms with tattoos, logos, or slogans like, "Don't walk behind me cause I might not be a good guide. Don't walk ahead of me cause I might not keep up. Don't walk alongside me, please. Just give me my space and leave me the hell alone."

The His and Hers section of this book is He and She comparisons. You'll find traditions scattered to the wind and legendary couples who will remain charred silhouettes scorched into your mind.

Love and marriage may go together like a horse and carriage, but the two people holding the reins control the vehicle. So, raise your champagne glass in a toast to the bride and groom.

What better words than those of Joan Crawford, who once said, "Love is a fire. But whether it is going to warm your heart or burn down your house, you can never tell."

HUSBAND

Marriage is not a game to be entered into lightly. Players consist of a husband and a wife, one of each is sufficient. The course is rough and sometimes tricky. Cowards, quitters or poor sports, beware! Marriage is not for you. The best equipment for this sport is love, honor, and a good sense of humor.

To whom it may concern. He is taken. There is a license somewhere to prove this fact. To the general public, he is banded with gold. This means, private property--keep out. In short, he is a husband.

As any wife can tell you, husbands vary in size, shape, and form. Out of hearing distance of her spouse she will readily admit she has the best of the species ensnared in her trap.

A husband is an overgrown boy poising as a man. His needs vary with his moods. For instances, he'd like a mother at home, wants a showgirl to take out on the town, needs a lady wizard to balance his budget, insists on a maid to do household tasks, and desires a mistress for obvious reasons.

If you are loaded with good looks, good measurements, brains, charm, patience, have a good disposition, and wonderful sense of humor, you may be lucky enough to fill the bill--all wrapped in one neat package labeled, wife. Most husbands like meals on time, you at home, skin-tight pants or dresses on other women, a good listener, socks without holes, no starch in his shorts, please! And, an occasional night out with the boys.

He forgets important dates like birthdays, anniversaries, and to tell you he's bringing a few guests home for dinner.

He dislikes overcooked meat, missing buttons, a bikini on his wife, cold feet in bed, an overdrawn checking account, discussion about buying anything that costs money, and company visiting when he's tired. In other words, he likes to rest and relax in his easy chair in front of the television with a snack, his newspaper, and you in that order.

In the due process of time, you hope, whether you whisper it gently in his ear or surprise him with a tiny bootie, he learns he is going to be a father. As you watch with expectation, he ranges from "Who me?" to "Oh, boy!" He picks you up and swings you around. Then, shocked by his actions, he gently places you on an uncertain pedestal for about the next seven months. He can't understand your easy tears, hearty appetite, or changing appearance. He's proud of you, but he'd just as soon you'd stick close to home.

He matures his whole nine months during that last mad dash to the hospital. After you've packed your bag, called the doctor and reassured him everything is A-okay, you're on your way to the hospital. As nature takes her course, he paces the waiting room, pesters the personnel, and smiles sickly at the old joke, "We haven't lost a father yet"

When he's wild-eyed with shock and down to his last finger nail, a nurse appears and calmly informs him, "You're a father!" This news finally sinks in as he looks through the nursery glass window at his son. The kid has his face and the best pair of lungs in the nursery.

Floating down the hall, he visits the sweetest, little mother in the world. After an ether kiss, with a promise to rest, he marches out to meet the world--chest out, shoulders up, and a silly-looking grin on his face. He passes out cigars like a one man army.

In the next few months, mom learns he dislikes dirty diapers, baby bottles, a messy house, getting up in the middle of the night to walk the floor with junior, and a woman that is more mother than wife. He varies between wondering if his heir is the smartest, cutest baby in the world, or if that kid will ever shut up crying!

Alas! You find you have two babies on your hands. Sleepily,

you wonder which one is the most trouble. Just as you are about to throw in the towel--which is dirty, of course--father shows his true colors. He takes junior, who has miraculously turned into a boy and makes him into an athlete, honor student, or both. You watch proudly as they troop off to collect their honors. You sigh and truly know, "It's a man's world!"

Hubby hates to fuss or fight. He will go to all lengths to avoid either. However, he blows up easily and tears out of the house leaving you to wonder, "What can I say that will be strong enough to shame the brute when he gets home this evening?"

Then, he breezes in, all smiles, with two tickets for that special show you wanted to see. He wonders why you seem so frosty around the edges. You look in the mirror at a frump with curlers in her hair, unplucked brows and wail, "I'll never get ready to go out tonight." All the while you're calling a sitter, fixing an early dinner for the kids, laying out your spouse's clothes, waiting for your turn at the bathroom, and wondering "what on earth am I going to wear?"

After he's honked for ten minutes, you give your hair a final pat, pull a run in your last pair of panty hose, and close the door on the sitter, the kids, and utter chaos. You paste on a smile and waltz out to meet your escort.

As you scoot in beside him, he snarls, "What took you so long? I've been ready for thirty minutes."

You grind your teeth, count to ten, and smile.

He grunts.

As you drive along, the years drift away. You cover the distance between you and him. Just as you've settled, he yelps, "For Pete's sake, quit crowding me. Can't you see the traffic's heavy here? Who do you think we are, two kids on a date?"

Taking a chance, you stay where you are and say, "Yes!"

Unexpectedly, he laughs. You join in. The two of you are acting like two crazy kids on a date.

During the course of the evening, you overhear someone say, "What a nice looking couple."

You discover they are talking about you two.

He smiles at you as if to say, "Hello beautiful."

And, suddenly, you are the most beautiful woman in the

room, to him! And, that's all that matters. You smile up at him-
-this unpredictable male. You realize he's still the handsome,
young giant, you promised to love, honor and cherish.

In your heart, you know, you wouldn't trade him for any
man on earth, this great, big, wonderful hunk of a man, you call
husband.

HEIRLOOMS

The Howard Hunt Johnson house on the corner of Benton and North Maple Street is a landmark home built in 1869 by Frank Furth of St. Louis.

Historically, the Johnson house was one of the first two-story houses in town. One of the things that set it apart was the ornamental, antique fence with spikes protruding upward, tempting kids to race along the sidewalk rat-a-tat-tatting a stick. However, dignity of the house was not conducive to this prank. Everyone knew the iron gate which opened easily was privy only to those with a calling card.

A manicured lawn hosted a sidewalk which unfurled like a red carpet leading to steps ascending to a wide, covered porch. Shrubbery was abundant.

The business section of town gradually approached the big house on the corner. My dad built a service station south of Johnson's. The station, bordering Johnson's lawn, was separated by a less ornamental fence.

When Howard Johnson walked up Maple Street toward his business, he passed Dad's station. If Dad were gassing a vehicle, Howard would wave. If the opportunity presented itself, Howard would stop for a short sidewalk visit.

I knew Mr. Johnson through my parents and later as a friend. He was always friendly, smiling, and courteous.

A little girl notices these things, but her eyes follow the lady of the house. Helen Marie Myers Johnson was a lady. She graced the Johnson home with dignity. A slender, fair-skinned, dark-haired, woman of fragile beauty, she was the beginning of a generation which would see women become a working force in the business world.

Helen gave of her time to community clubs, school and church, entertainment in her home, and on occasion found time to be hostess at the family drug store.

My cousin worked part-time at their business during her high school years. Before her marriage, the Johnson family hosted a trousseau shower in their home. A tea affair provided refreshments, background music, and a display of gifts, and garments from her wedding trousseau. I had been inside the Johnson house, but this event transformed the home into a fairyland for marriage. Perhaps this was "mode of the day" but it was new to our set. The affair was mimicked but never quite so graciously.

Howard and Helen had one son, Charles (Chuck) Johnson. He was their life. Howard introduced him to the world of sports. Helen raised her son as a gentleman. The combination of culture produced an outstanding athlete, who became a lawyer.

Years became a whirlwind of family and career activities as my generation became the responsible adults.

One day the town mourned as Helen Marie Myers Johnson passed away. Her absence left an empty space never quite filled. Howard kept the house, minimized the business, doted on his grandchildren, and searched for the easy friendship visiting days that were quickly becoming a thing of the past.

One day Howard slipped quietly away to join his wife.

Recently, I passed the Johnson house and was amazed at the bustle of activity that accompanies an estate sale. The sale had progressed to the back yard. Purchases of the day were scattered over what had once been an immaculate lawn. The front gate stood ajar welcoming those whose calling card was media advertising of the sale. I circled the block wishing my day had been free to attend and purchase a keepsake.

Standing by the front steps, as if ascending the stairs to make a social call, was an older lady. She stood, staring blankly, as people rushed helter-skelter past her. Perhaps, she was remembering the good old days and the genteel family who had resided at this heirloom residence.

I drove away letting my mind take me where reality would never step foot again. My keepsakes will not be treasurers laid up where dust and moth can corrupt or thieves break through to steal, but memories giving me instant access to the grand old days of yesteryear and the memory of a real gentleman, Howard Hunt Johnson.

GOTTA KNOW WHEN YOU HOLD UP

"Sorry to break up the card game, guys, but it's my wife's birthday and I've got a present for her." Stud wiggled his pelvis in an Elvis imitation as he headed for the door.

"Think his wife will settle for that?" Jonesy asked.

"Sure, after he gives her the diamond ring he bought her."

"Why can't a woman just be satisfied with a man's loving?" Jonesy wondered.

"You telling us your wife would be satisfied with just you for a birthday gift?" We all hooted.

"Use to be, before I popped the question, she accepted, and we tied the knot." Jonesy pondered his statement. "After we got married, everything changed."

"How's that?" T. J., the youngest edition to the card game asked. He was shacked up with a good-looking redhead named Lovie who didn't seem to mind his nights out with the guys.

"When they say 'I do' to you at the alter, it alters everything. Ain't long until the only way you can get them in the mood for loving is for you to answer 'I do' when they ask, 'Want to take me shopping?'"

T. J. smirked, "That'll be the day."

Before the year was over T. J. married Lovie. His card games were few and far between for awhile. After about six months, he started showing up on a regular basis.

"How's your love life, T. J.?" Jonesy asked as he raked in another pile of chips.

"It's on hold," T. J. said.

"How's that?" Jonesy asked.

"About two weeks ago, Lovie and I turned in early. She snuggled up and I got excited. But, when I started getting amorous, she said, 'I'm not in the mood, T. J. Why don't you just hold me.'"

"'Hold you,' I says, 'I'll hold you, but I got other things on my mind, too.'"

The guys hooted and cheered.

"What happened?" Jonesy asked.

"Lovie turned cold as a iced watermelon. She turned her back, and said, 'T. J. you just aren't in tune with my emotions as a lady.'"

"What'd you do?" Jonesy asked.

"Hell, I held her. According to her emotions nothing else was available. What else could I do?"

Jonesy chuckled, "Take her shopping, maybe."

T. J. raised his eyebrows as he laid down a full house. "Seems shopping was on her mind 'cause the next night she was after me to GO TO THE MALL.

"Did you go?"

"Sure, I followed her through every department of the most expensive store in the mall. I watched her try on five different things. She fussed and fumed and couldn't make up her mind. Finally, she asked me with a pretty pout, "T. J. you choose, which one do you think I should get?"

"Hell, honey, you look good enough to eat in all of them. Why don't you just buy them all?"

Jonesy exclaimed, "What a generous man you are, T. J."

"I guess Lovie thought the same thing cause she decided she needed matching shoes for everything."

Jonesy snickered, "That'll be the day, you say?"

"Yep, after the shoes, she leads me to the make-up counter and decides on a complete line of make up to go with her new outfits."

"What'd you do?"

"I just smiled and kept following her around the store with her cart filling up at every turn. Finally, she purred, 'Honey, I'm ready to go to the checkout. Are you sure you can afford all this?'" You should have seen the expression on her face when I said, 'I'm not in the mood to buy all this stuff. Why don't you just hold it?'"

Jonesy hooted.

"'Hold it? Are you crazy? I've just picked out the perfect outfits. You know how long it took to find shoes to match these outfits? And, the makeup!'" Lovie was drawing a crowd. "'I must admit I played to the crowd shamelessly. But, it felt soooo good when I said, 'Lovie, you must not be in tune with my emotional and monetary needs as a man.'"

The card game stopped and the guys actually applauded T. J.

He grinned, "You should have heard the applause I got from the men in the crowd while their wives clucked sympathetically with Lovie."

"So, you never did answer my question, T. J." Jonesy reminded him after the laughter subsided and the game resumed.

"What was it, Jonesy?"

"How's your love life?"

"Let's put it this way, Jonesy. You can count on me as a regular member of the card club for awhile. 'Cause, in cards as well as marriage, you got to know when to hold 'em and know when to fold 'em. Right now Lovie's folding and I'm holding.

Jane and Rex Shewmaker

THE WARMTH OF MEMORIES

I sit here in the dark trying to remember what we did when I was growing up back in the Ozarks when the electricity was off.

If Saturday had been a beautiful day and my brother and I were able to play outside with the neighborhood kids, we generally looked forward to a Sunday of the same kind of activity. But, if the weather man on the radio, our main source of weather news, should forecast an icy day ahead, we usually agreed with Dad, who scoffed, "That weather man never did know what he was talking about."

If, however, we awoke to find ourselves buried deep in covers, which mom had tucked securely around us during the night, and looked to the windows searching for sunshine, only to find a lacy residue of white doilies patterned there, we crawled, reluctantly, from our individual cozy cocoons, and hurried to the fragrance of the kitchen where mom was busy preparing breakfast.

Dad's chair, tilted to rest on the two back legs, supported him precariously, as he buried himself in the depths of the Sunday newspaper. Waiting until his face appeared when he prepared to turn a page in search of more news, I'd venture, "Looks like that old weather man knows a thing or two about a thing or two, eh dad?"

Dad grinned. "Everybody gets lucky once in awhile."

Icy days weren't as much fun outside as snowy days because we could only slide so much before falling down. Snow days were made for sleds and building snowmen and snow ice cream. Icy days, whether the Lord's day or not, required work to prepare the house for evenings, which brought in dropping temperatures. At those times, our home needed more warmth. Family stands out like a bright spot in my memory when I recall housebound evenings with the wind whipping at the windows and old man winter knocking on the door. Dad always kept kerosene lanterns stored for emergencies like a power outage from ice on electric lines.

Warmth comes from togetherness. Huddled at the kitchen table with the lantern casting a golden glow across the table, we'd pull out a game board like Monopoly, checkers, the Chinese checker board, or a card game, and we'd spend the winter evening laughing, joking, teasing, and trying our hand at friendly-family cheating as we passed the popcorn bowl around and around the table. Bottled beverages were a thing in the future, but our home had a surplus of good, cold, water if we wanted to venture to the back porch to refill glasses.

Stoking the heat stove for the evening and storing extra wood in the wood box, we'd ready ourselves for bed secure in the knowledge sunshiny days were ahead.

Now, the memory of family fun in the Ozarks, as I remember it, surfaces on cold, icy evenings when the power is out and one needs to draw on memories to keep one warm.

SECTION V
E very Man

Father Images

FATHER IMAGES

Every man is the one man to someone. This segment is dedicated to that special man in someone's life. I asked friends and family to honor their fathers by writing a tribute for this part of Every Day Is Father's Day. My request was to write a short, tight, paragraph on this subject, What I'd like to say to my father but never have.

A special thanks to those who honored their fathers and to the men whose stories appear as examples of heroes, mentors, and Father Images.

John Macdonnell, Farmer/Business owner

What I wish I'd said to my Dad, Dr. T. M. Macdonnell, and never have...."

I'm not perfect. Far from it. Everyone has vices and I know I have a few of my own, but over the years I have learned something from my father which offset my faults and allowed me to be who I am. It is what I consider to be the code by which I live.

"Integrity is doing the right thing, even when no one's looking."

Dad is someone of the highest character of whom I give my total respect. I have seen him in times, good and bad, do what needed to be done because it was the right thing to do. Living as he's taught me, I can walk with my head high. The integrity

I've attained means as with everyone at those times when I am looked upon in judgment I can say with confidence that anyone who knows me may be asked at random of the state of my character and that's a good enough defense for me.

For these qualities he's instilled in me I can say this:
Dad, it worked. I've grown up. I don't always make the right choices, and even sometimes when I do you may not understand or agree with them, but you've taught me to stick to my guns, and I am better for it. You can trust me that what I do is right and good, for what you have done before me is right and good. There's a big difference between being male and being a Man, and thanks to you, I know I am a Man, and as a Man I can say to my father, "I love you."

✳ ✳ ✳ ✳

Edsel Matthews, coach/Athletic Administrator

Dear Dad,

This is more of a thank you letter. It is one of the things I wish I had said to you but never did.

Dad, you were forty-six years old and coaching basketball at Southwest Missouri State when you died without warning from a heart attack. You were a tremendous loss to our family, your many friends, and fans in Southwest Missouri.

You were the perfect role model for me personally and professionally, so much that I followed in your foot steps into coaching and athletic administration. There are many things that I wish I could have asked you about as I traveled through my career. I was twenty-three when you passed.

Dad, I want to thank you for being such a wonderful Christian example and setting the highest of ethical standards both personally and professionally.

I respect you more than anyone and have always wanted to be like you and not disappoint you. I think of you every day and have tired to emulate what I believe you would have wanted me to do.

Besides saying thank you for my professional philosophy, I want to express my gratitude to you for introducing me to the great outdoors. I love the land, conservation, hunting, and fishing.

The Matthews men have always had a fondness for cattle. I want to thank you and my grandfather, Charlie Matthews, for introducing me to the cattle business.

Lastly, I wish you could have known your grandchildren and great-grandchildren. You would have loved them and been very proud of them.

> Your son,
> Edsel Matthews

Shirleen Sando, Publisher and Producer

"My father was the jewel of my soul, the sparkle in my eyes, and the courage in my spine, and while he is gone, he remains that today."

John J. Sweeney, Remodeling Concepts

Dad,
Sorry our friendship ended so soon in life
you, fifty-nine, and me, twenty-one.
But in the last twenty-one years,
in business and life,
it's simple to see
it's still you and me.
— Johnny Jack

৵ ৵ ৵ ৵

Bill Vaughan, President, Bank of Urbana

Dear Dad,
I wish I had told you how much I respected your judgment,
how much I hope to live my life with the same principles you
lived yours, and I wish I could tell you that I think of you each
and every day.
Love, Bill

৵ ৵ ৵ ৵

"The older I got, the smarter he got."
Ronald Mason, Retired Engineer

৵ ৵ ৵ ৵

**F. Mark Day,
Classmate, 1952**

My dad was a First Christian Church pastor. His major in college was history with a divinity minor, so his sermons were based on biblical history.

If he were here today, I would tell him how his sermons made me aware of the times the Bible was written and I am very critical of ministers that preach without a real understanding of the intent of a verse or chapter because they do not know the history of the society of that time.

I thank him for that.

è&   è&   è&   è&

Dusty Richards, Western Writer

Who doesn't have things unsaid to a departed parent? Stand up and raise your hand. You are the exception then. My father never felt any pain. I mean things that would disable most of us, he never experienced. So his concern for a son that wasn't as fortunate meant he scoffed at his complaints and went on. If you didn't keep up, you faced his impatience. The years went by, and I wanted to tell him,–"Listen you never hurt, and I do," but the chance never came. Now he's gone, and I never found the space to fit it in. Maybe it wasn't important. I'm glad he never suffered.

è&   è&   è&   è&

Michael Garrett, The Book Doctor

Thank you, Dad, for your service to our country. You never talked much about your war experiences until your final days and I was too overwhelmed by losing you at that time to stop and think about what you endured to keep us free. When I was a kid, I idolized super-heroes like Superman, Batman, etc., but I now know that as a child I lived under the same roof with a very special super-hero. I miss you.

ૐ ૐ ૐ ૐ

Tamara Hanson, Author, *Mastering The Dance*

My father, a giant of a man, was far too rough and tough to rear girls, but rear them he did. He endured stockings slung over the shower curtain and what he referred to as "dainties" on the towel racks of the bathroom we all shared. However, he drew the line at any shirking of duties.

Despite much grousing, we girls learned skills usually reserved to boys. My sister and I can fix a toilet, rewire a lamp, hammer a nail straight, drain a hot water heater, and repair a garden hose. We can problem-solve a sprinkler system and mow a lawn on the diagonal. Handy men jury rig a repair job at their own peril.

Maybe I'm lucky he didn't have sons after all.

ૐ ૐ ૐ ૐ

Marilyn Smith, Columnist and feature writer

Now that I am older and wiser I can more easily appreciate the benefits I reaped by picking up rock by the hour, baling hay in the hot sun, slopping the ole smelly hogs, gathering the eggs from under pecking chickens, weeding the garden and all the other farm chores I was expected to do. But now that I am older and wiser my father is not here to thank for instilling the work ethic in me. Every aspect of my life has been molded by his honesty, curiosity, mischief, and values. I would not be the person I am today had it not been for him.

≈   ≈   ≈   ≈

Rex Shewmaker, Businessman

If I could say something to Dad that I never said it would be thanks. I'm not sure if I ever thanked him for everything he did for me.

Dad, thanks for giving me the time and opportunity to participate in sports. Your support was a big help to me both in school sports and in independent ball.

Thanks for the things you taught me in business and for acting like you didn't notice when I'd go to the post office for the mail and stop off at Bud Henderson's station, the meeting place for my friends, and sit in on a game of checkers or cards.

Thanks for the meals we shared across the street at Uncle Gene's café where family and friends would stop by our table to visit. And, thanks for paying for the meal!

It's easy to take things for granted when you're working with your dad daily in a business as we did, first on the farm, and later as partners in Shewmaker Auto Parts. It's easy to think he'll always be around. Until your dad's gone you don't realize there were things you never said to him. Dad, you probably know the things I left unsaid. You seem to always know everything else I didn't get around to telling you. Did I ever tell you I love you? Well, I did and I do.

Your son, Rex

≈   ≈   ≈   ≈

Thomas Rex Shewmaker, Businessman

Dad, Aunt Jane asked me what I wish I'd said to you and never did. I told her since you're still around, I'll have the opportunity to say it to you, so here goes.

Thanks is a big part of what I'd like to say to you, just like you did to your dad, my papa Blaine.

Thanks for being my father and coach who always supported me, my brothers and sisters, and a lot of the teams in school, town, and community sports. Your love of sports was contagious. I think we all caught it. Thanks for the time you spent teaching my kids sports and attending their games. Even more than sports, I think your love for competition made life exciting. Thanks for teaching us that losing was not an option.

Thanks for the things you've taught me in business while we worked together at the family business, Shewmaker Auto Parts. Thanks for the times you'd say, "You better take off if you're going to make that game."

There's a lot of things I'd like to say to you. Hopefully, we'll both be around for a long time. Maybe I'll get them all said.

Love, Tom

          èa   èa   èa   èa

Robert Vaughan, Author, *Brandywine's War: Back in Country*

I am a writer, and I work at home. For the last couple of years of my dad's life, he would come by, every day, to interrupt my work. "I know you are writing, so I won't stay long," he would say. What he didn't realize was that it didn't matter whether he stayed long or not . . . once the writing rhythm was interrupted, it would take me an hour or longer to get back into the groove.

How I miss those 'interruptions,' now. And, how I wish I had told him, then, "Dad, you can stay as long as you want. It can never be too long."

➴ ➴ ➴ ➴

Betty Craker Henderson, Author and Entertainer

It is truly a blessing to know that I am one of the lucky ones who was able to always talk with my father about anything. He has been gone for seventeen years this spring, but there is nothing that I regret not having discussed with him in the past. He was a wonderful man and the circumstances of his own childhood made him treasure his family above anything else, and he conveyed that to his children. Now, if I want to share a special moment, I address it to the winds that circle the earth and know it will be carried to him by God's own messengers.

➴ ➴ ➴ ➴

Doug Gabriel, Branson Star and Entertainer

"Dad, thank you for being such a wonderful father to me. You have shown me how to be a good dad, husband, and friend. You are my hero and will always be the wind beneath my wings! I love you always! And forever and thank you for being my rock."

Love, Your son Doug

➴ ➴ ➴ ➴

Mary Davis, Head Kitchen Coach Time Out Café

My Dearest Daddy,

Even though you've been gone for several years now, you are in my thoughts often every day.

Growing up I could go to you with every problem and every joy in my life. When I made a bad decision, you were there to hold my hand and let me cry on your shoulder. When I did good, you rooted the loudest and longest of everyone.

All the camping, fishing, and hunting, we did taught me patience and that silence is not a bad thing.

I will never stop loving or missing you.

Mary

 za za za za

Kyndall Warford, Junior at Buffalo High School 2006

Dear Daddy,

You've always been there for me even when I was wrong. You punished me when I was bad but in a loving, stern way. I told you I would take good care of you when I was young, and I stick by my promises. I may get mad at you from time to time but you'll always know I love you. When I was little, you were my hero, and I thought you were immortal. I still think of you as my hero but with each passing day I know your health is giving out. But, you're still my hero. You once told me if you love someone tell them as much as you can. Sometimes, I don't let you know, but I'm telling you now.

I love you, Daddy.

Your little girl, Kyndall

za za za za

Terry Dan Stevens, Retired Military

You know, Dad, we should have been brothers. When I reached the age you were when I was born, I finally learned what it meant to be responsible for a family. When my first grandchild was born, I realized the family link to the future was secure. You made me proud of my family name and mother made me proud of hers. You were carefree and a bit reckless when a youth as was I. When you retired, you did so with honor and a lifetime of success, as did I. For a couple of people who for years thought they had nothing in common, it turns out that we had everything in common—except the capacity to reveal our inner selves to each other.

ૐ ૐ ૐ ૐ

Janet L. Basnett, Business Woman

Dad had cancer. He was not expected to live longer than six months; however, he beat the odds and lived for another five and a half years. He was in a lot of pain, but he hardly ever complained. He was brave and strong right up to the night he took his last breath.

A few months earlier, I did have the blessed opportunity to tell my dad how much I loved him and how thankful I was to have him for a father. Also I told him how happy I was that he and mother had taken us children to church when we were small and taught us about the Lord.

I wish I could have told my dad before he was gone how strong he became to me even after the sickness had smothered the life slowly out of his body. He was so frail and so weak from not eating, and yet he held on like a true soldier through the toughest battle.

If he were here today, I would overwhelm him with kisses and hugs and lots of attention and tell him everyday just how much he meant to me. I felt so rich knowing him. I possess riches untold, even after he is gone because of what he gave me in love, happiness and hope. He was a great storyteller, and he made everyone laugh and children loved him. He left us a legacy that we will never forget.

"I love you, Dad," Janet.

ક્ષ   ક્ષ   ક્ષ   ક્ષ

Barri L. Bumgarner, Author

In all the years I looked up to you, I didn't understand your need to internalize everything stress-related. And so you immersed them in a bottle. No one knew in those early years how deep the problem would burrow. Perhaps we could've stopped you. If I knew then what I know now, I would have screamed from the mountain tops, "STOP!" When I was ten or twelve, a simple declaration might have made all the difference. Something simply profound like, "I'm proud of who you are, Daddy, and you don't have to drink to soak up the stress. Let us help."

Maybe it would've mattered.

ક્ષ   ક્ષ   ક્ષ   ક્ષ

Charlotte Eidlin, Administrator Social Development Research Group University of Washington

A MIGHTY TREE

I always thought of my dad as the epitome of strength. He wasn't a big man; however, he had a tremendous spiritual strength, a faith in the God that is bigger than we are and that will take care of us.

It was the small things that I remember most about him, picking blackberries so Mom could make my favorite pie when I came home from wherever I lived or sending pecans that he had shelled and bagged from his pecan trees in the yard. Those pecans were always much better than any from the local grocery store. I looked forward to them every year as I knew he had picked them from the yard and shelled every one at the kitchen table. Sometimes he also sent some still in the shell. I have part of a bag of unshelled pecans in my freezer that have moved with me from Texas to Ohio to Washington. It is like having a part of the "Mighty Tree" with me wherever I go.

❧   ❧   ❧   ❧

MY AUNT'S STORY
Joyce Lynn Sadler Winter

In the heat of the late spring, I'd watch from the kitchen window as my father plowed the field and planted crops with the help of his mules. From a distance, I could see his khaki shirt soaked with perspiration, and I also noticed he'd stop the mules every so often, take off his old, dirty, worn hat and swipe his sweat soaked brow, using his long sleeved shirt. I promised myself: "One day, when I grow bigger, I am going to help my dad with the sowing and planting and take some of the hard work off him." When I became older, I did fulfill the promise I had made to myself. I wish I had told my father a few years before what I had been dreaming of for so long.

FAMILY STYLE

Family style is a continuation of the Every Man section with other authors writing about their fathers. The following selections are stories rather than paragraphs.

In long hand, on a 6 x 9 Springfield writing tablet, my mother, Inez Sadler Shewmaker, wrote a history in 1985 which she titled, "Family Style." I found it among some of her things and consider it her contribution to this book. D. T. Strawn is my maternal great grandfather. Ed Sadler is my maternal grandfather.

The last selections in Family style are by the author.

ิ   ิ   ิ   ิ

MY MOTHER'S STORY
Inez Sadler Shewmaker

Ed and Georgia Sadler and a little family of two daughters, Inez and Argeree, lived in the boothills of the Arbuckle mountains, near Davis, Oklahoma.

This family enjoyed the outdoors of fresh air and the God-given sunshine. This was a very healthy family whose mother canned from a garden made by her husband, who had a knack for making gardens in nice straight rows.

Ed was a man quick in actions on anything he undertook to do. He worked for a man with a lot of land to attend and in those days just horses and mules to work with. Toiling the soil on Mr. White's large farms and caring for the stock, cows, calves, horses and mules, Ed made a good hired hand. His motto was "Get to work ten minutes before time to start and remain ten minutes after time to stop."

At the end of a hard day's work, tired in body, feet hurting from following behind a plow or disk all day walking in clods of dirt, Ed would meet Mr. White, smile, and tip his hat as they discussed how the working of the soil was going.

"I'll be back at ten till seven in the morning," Ed promised as he began walking the two miles home to the little house furnished them by Mr. White.

Home at last, Ed walked into the house where the smell of something good cooking perked him up. Then there was a dash by his two little girls as they each grabbed their father's legs, making it hard for him to walk as they hung on. His daughters were all cleaned up for their dad with little starched dresses and bloomers.

Ed and Georgia Sadler had a love for each other and their family. Today we seldom see this kind of love. But they disciplined their daughters as Inez learned when her father teased her about a hired hand on Mr. White's farm. Inez, with a hot temper, threw her fork, hitting her father between the eyes. He spanked her but teased her no more.

A few years later Ed rented a farm near Satterwhite, Oklahoma, where he toiled the soil planting cotton and other grain. Another daughter, Ella Mae, was born and grew to walking age. She was in everything. Ed set some steel traps to catch animals. While the family was picking cotton, Ella Mae was playing and got caught in one of the steel traps. Ed stopped picking cotton and got his daughter out of the steel trap, consoling her crying while the rest of the family felt a deep hurt for Ella Mae's misfortune. Then, the family continued their cotton picking.

Inez and Argeree walked two miles to attend Satterwhite School. Often Inez and Argeree rode their dad's riding horse. One day while riding up a steep hill they heard a sound above them in the air. They were afraid when they looked up and saw a winged object. They hurried the horse on home to tell their mom and dad. Their parents ask them if they had seen the plane in the air? This was the first airplane they had ever seen.

The Ed Sadler family moved to Alpers, Oklahoma, where Ed struggled to purchase a forty acre farm of his own. Realizing he needed some help, he went into partnership with his wife's parents, D. T. and Caroline Strawn.

The Sadlers and Strawns lived in a house on the farm near another building close to the highway which soon became a grocery store and post office. Ed attended the farm work and Grandpa Strawn, with the help of his daughter, Georgia, attended the store and post office.

Grandma Strawn churned the cream from the cow's milk and made butter and buttermilk.

The house had a fireplace in the living room. Grandma Strawn raked coals from the fire out on the hearth. She set her iron skillet on them with lard from the hogs which had been killed and rendered for fat. When the lard was hot in the skillet, Grandma Strawn spooned her mixture of mush into the hot grease and let it cook. As she was doing this, the three girls would come through the house and say, "Grandma, what are your making?"

Grandma would say, "Hush, I'm making mush."

That would make the girls laugh cause Grandma had made a rhyme.

Ed Sadler had a lot of old sayings like these.

I could stretch a mile if it wasn't for walking back.

Water, water, water Jack, you should have been there and half way back.

When asked, "Daddy, was I there?" Ed would say, "No, daughter. But, you were on the road somewhere."

ᕦ ᕦ ᕦ ᕦ

THE GIFTS MY FATHER GAVE ME
Jory Sherman, Author

My father, Keith Edward Sherman, gave me so many gifts during his seventy-seven years of life that I wonder why I never thanked him while he was alive. I have thanked him, mentally, many times since his death, and I have the strange feeling that he, with his living soul, can hear me.

Born in 1892, my father might have posed for those Calvert ads labeled "A Man of Distinction." He was an imposing figure with but a sixth grade education. Yet, he read to my sister Kay and me from books he kept as treasures in his library. He read Owen Wister's *The Virginian*, along with Napoleon Hill's *Think and Grow Rich*, and my great Aunt B. M. Bowers' western novels, among them *Good Indian* and *Chip of the Flying U*. Aunt Bert was my grandmother's sister, Bertha Muzzy, who wrote under that pseudonym.

When I was old enough, Dad asked me to take out a library card, which was another of his gifts to me. "Books," he said, "let you meet the greatest minds of history. The library is your entrance into the world of knowledge." I have never forgotten what he told me, and I have passed it along to my children and to those in schools where I have talked about my profession as a writer.

Dad gave me lists of books he wanted to read. He was a self-educated man, and before he went into a business venture, he always read scores of books so that he became an expert on everything from manufacturing to lumber. I read those books he had me withdraw and so gained some knowledge of the pyramids, the lumber industry, manufacturing, hunting, fishing, and golf.

I caddied for my father, who greatly admired Bobby Jones, and shot in the 80s, the high 70s. I watched him play golf with both admiration and envy. He was ambidextrous, so played golf left-handed, and I could never use his clubs. I eventually had to buy my own because I loved the game.

He loved horses and the outdoor life. He gave me my first horse, a little cow pony named Sugar, when I was eight years old. He also gave me my first gun, a Winchester 28 gauge shotgun. He was a great wing shooter. I learned from him because we often hunted quail, pheasant, ducks and geese together.

Once, when we were hunting ring-necked pheasants in the wheat fields that surrounded our home in Colorado, he was walking a ridge to my left, while I was down on the flat. A cock pheasant broke cover and took wing. We both hunted for that pheasant in the shorn wheat field and finally, my dad said, "Let's go on, then, do some more hunting." "But I want to find my pheasant," I said. "Your pheasant?" he said as we both looked at each other.

"Did you shoot?" We had both fired together, and I'll never know which of us downed that pheasant. But, I have a strong hunch that it wasn't me.

He told me, "Never retire from the work you love to do. Those men who sit on the porch in their rocking chairs fall over dead." When he retired, I saw the change in him. His restless mind drove him to act as a consultant to other business men, so he did not sit on that rocking chair. He died peacefully in his sleep at my brother Keith's home in College Station, Texas. I was on a new Harley motorcycle, a 74cc, full dress machine, heading for Texas to see him. When my sister, Sunny Lynn, told me that he had died, we were in Carlsbad Caverns with my wife Charlotte, and my son Frank, who was riding a BMW. When we left that morning, I felt my father's presence in the wind against my face, in the scent of the dew rising from the barren New Mexico landscape. I wrote an article for a motorcycle magazine about that experience, which was published by *Road Rider* magazine in their first issue. It was called "Summer End," and maybe it was my way of thanking my father for all the gifts he had given me.

He instilled in me a lifelong love of books and a thirst and hunger for learning. That was his strongest gift to me. But, he also gave me his love, which was the greatest gift of all. Over the years, I have tried to pass that love along to my own children.

Are you listening, Dad? I thank you, and I love you.

୫   ୫   ୫   ୫

BIGGEST MAN IN MY WORLD
Vicki Cox

My father, Hiram L. Jenkins, was the biggest, strongest person in my world. He could push my swing so high the chains went limp before I arched back to the ground. His grab on the merry-go-round sent me spinning faster than anybody else's father could. He taught me how to dive and was there grabbing me up out of the bubbles when I dared jump off the high board.

No wonder he was the person we went to for the big jobs. He renovated the majestic mansions in St. Louis, carrying out rotting timbers and wrestling new dry wall into place. He painted our house by himself, dipping the biggest, thickest brush in the paint and lathering it on the walls. He built a garage and renovated a railroad station that had been gutted by fire. He took the grimy, mundane, tedious jobs nobody else wanted and turned them into something worthy. He crawled under the house with the bugs and spiders (and sometimes snakes) to repair some pipe or wiring. On the golf course, he'd wade into the brush and find lost balls no one else could--and usually discovered a few someone else had given up trying to find.

My dad was a gifted craftsman. He could take a knotted, rough cut plank of cherry or walnut wood and turn it into something beautiful. He designed clocks, magazine footstools, and crèches for our Nativity figurines. When I couldn't find a bookshelf large enough for my picture albums, he made one for me. He built walnut cedar chests for his granddaughters and a walnut TV center for his grandson. He rubbed and oiled them until the grain glowed.

The heat might cling to us like a second skin, but every weekend he took mother, my brother, and me to play nine holes at the local golf course. We'd whack and slap at the ball--mostly missing it. He'd encourage us with, "You're closing in on it." or "You're down to the short strokes." Then he'd address the ball with a three wood. He'd swing the club back as far as it would go, and then arc it down and up, his weight shifting into it. The motion was pure grace.

He kept playing golf even when he had emphysema. He'd leave the oxygen tank in the car, and we'd head around the front nine. Because I played so ineptly, we'd let a foursomes play through us. I'll never forget the last time he swung a golf club. A foursome of young executive types played through us at the eighth hole and moved down the fairway to their balls. I took my turn at the ladies' tee. My drive bounced about 35 feet from the tee. Then Dad stepped up to the men's tee, put his head down, and swung. He out drove the young pups ahead of us, and we had to yell "Fore" to warn them. They ducked and then walked off, shaking their heads that a man in his seventies possessed that kind of power.

He was game for anything. He'd say, "If you're waiting on me, you're wasting your time." In 1991 when we flew to Hawaii to celebrate Pearl Harbor's 50th Anniversary, the family drove to a sandy beach to swim in the Pacific. He jumped in too. If the kids floated on a water park's wave pool, he'd be in the middle on his own inner tube, laughing, waving and sun burning the tops of his feet. If we wanted pork steaks for Christmas dinner, he'd barbecue them in the snow and the cold. Once, his grandchildren wanted to go fishing with him on the farm where we lived. He obligingly took them to the pond, even though on this particular August day, it was the wrong time of day to fish, and a gray haze hung over the water like a soggy blanket. After a while, his grandson, Nathan, ran back through the high grass, yelling, "Granddad caught a fish! Granddad caught a fish!" From a pond that supposedly held only blue gill, he hooked a catfish big enough to feed six for supper that night. I took his picture holding the cooked fish in the dining room. Lizabeth, his granddaughter, sat on his lap. Both beamed from ear to ear. You couldn't tell who was happier.

He had a repertoire of wise cracks and pet phrases. In the nursing home, an aide would come take his vital signs and ask how he was. He'd answer, smiling, "If I was any better, I couldn't stand it."

"I'll give you just twelve hours to stop that," he'd say when I put lotion on his back. If I told him of some success I'd had, he'd likely say, "Bea-ut-a-mous" or "Well, hoop-de-dee."

Dad was a simple man, but he was wiser than we gave him credit for. About midway in his fight against his emphysema, he and I were sitting at the kitchen table after playing cards all evening. I grumbled about the silliness of such games. He looked at me and said, "Why not? We're just marking time, anyway." Our eyes met. We both knew he wasn't talking about a game.

He spent many days in the hospital as his body began failing him. The last time I saw him, he was in the hospital bed, hooked to oxygen, IVs, and a heart monitor. But his spirit flew like a flag over the room. That day turned out to be a gift to us. His cheeks were rosy; he ate well. He wasn't wheezing. I told him a joke. He laughed, his eyes bright. He was my Dad again.

Now, Dad was not perfect. He could tell the biggest whoppers, yarns, and tall tales in three states. Before he became housebound, he'd have coffee at the local restaurant to kibitz with his friends. Hard telling what world crises he told them he had solved. I never knew when he started a story how much of it was true, how much he had lifted from a movie, or how much came from his imagination. It didn't matter. The story might be outlandish or extravagant, but it was a work of art.

I always wondered about his tall tales. His life needed no embellishments. He survived Pearl Harbor and served in the South Pacific. Flying bombing missions over Romania, he was shot down. Parachuting to safety, he injured his knee. Taken prisoner by the Germans, he carried a crewman on his back as they were marched from one location to another. He showed the stuff he was made of before he was twenty-one years old. We treasure the Purple Heart and commendations he received for his valor.

But Hiram L. Jenkins was more than a survivor of an historical event that happened a half century ago. He didn't have school diplomas or degrees, but he was uniquely gifted. He paid his dues in order to volunteer. He didn't have any money, but he was generous of heart. Despite how others treated him, he was patient and polite. He was my dad, a man who lived his life in little bits and pieces, sometimes at the fuzzy edge of my consciousness. Yet, I could always depend on him and on his love. He was my hero--and he always will be.

Right now, he's not gasping for breath, or choking, or coughing. He's breathing the clear, holy air of heaven. He's doing it in great easy gulps. And I know if he can play golf with angels, he'll be keeping score.

❆ ❆ ❆ ❆

LIFE WITHOUT FATHER
Frances Massey
Fashion Merchandiser, Web Designer

I have few vivid memories of my father that I know are my memories, not stories told about him as I grew up. How do I know this? Because no one else remembers these events. I was four and one-half years old when my father died. Since I was the youngest of the family, I was home with my father, a farmer, while my mother, brother and sister were at school.

I have one particularly vivid memory of riding down our farm lane with Daddy on our tractor. I was sitting between his legs, and he let me pretend to steer the tractor. Another memory is of the two of us in our pick-up truck driving over to his father's farm a few miles away. There was no one else with us. It was just the two of us for a few brief, precious moments in my young life with the man I would get to know through other people's stories and memories of him.

He was a good, solid man who loved his family, his land and his Ozarks surroundings. He was as grounded in the Ozarks as the oak and sycamore trees that filled his woods and riverbanks. I have often pondered the unanswerable questions about what my life would have been like if he had lived until I was an adult. What path would my own life adventure have taken with his direct influence on me?

My life path took me away from the Ozark Hills when I was twenty-one. I moved about as far away as possible, both literally and figuratively, to New York City. I loved being there and succeeded in my chosen career, but I always found my way back to my roots for all the special occasions. That's where I am from and where my father and forefathers are from. It's my heritage and a place I know I can always go home to, my father's home.

My father was liked and admired by many, so I'm told. My mother told me his funeral was overflowing with all the people who knew him from all around. She didn't even know who most of the people were. His name was David Lane Massey, but he was known as Lane or Pete, a nickname given to him by a hired hand on his father's farm when he was younger. I was given his middle name as my middle name, too, and he gave me his looks, his build, his mannerisms, and his sense of humor. Some of these things I can easily tell by looking at pictures of him and the others, I've been told by others as I grew up, "Why Frances, you stand just like your father did!" or "That is just how your father would say that joke!" That's not to say I don't have lots of influences from my mother (that would be another whole story!) but from my looks, there is no denying that I come from my father.

So, with all this history of him all my life, it still begs the question--how would my life have been different if he had lived to my adulthood? He was a farmer and was building up our farm and acquiring more land to expand his beef herd. His father's farm was only a few miles down the road, and he helped to farm it also. He would have acquired this farm in time. He loved to hunt and fish the Ozark woods and rivers. He loved good horses and was building a good line of walking horses with his father.

After his death, my mother sold the farm, and we moved into town where she got a good teaching job. She couldn't manage the farm, raise three young kids and work full time too. So, I grew up in town, not roaming the fields and woods of the farm. This is the first major change to my life without my father. Town and farm life are very different, even in a small rural Missouri town. Would I have still moved away to New York City to pursue my chosen career? Would my chosen career even have been the same? These are questions I would like to be able to talk to my father about today. What would have been his advice and influence on me at that time of my life.

College was in the picture for me regardless of my father being alive or not. We were groomed to go to college from birth by both our parents. I attended the University of Missouri, as did my brother and sister before me. My chosen studies, fashion merchandising, took me away from Missouri. There isn't much call for clothing designing in Missouri. I'm told he would have encouraged me to pursue any of my dreams. Under his personal guidance, would I have had the same dream? I will never know.

As a young girl, I always assumed I would marry a nice young man and have kids and follow the "American Dream." Well, I did marry a nice young man, but the path was not what I visualized as a young girl. We didn't have a big family wedding. In fact, we didn't have a traditional wedding at all. We went to the justice of peace for a quiet ceremony and told everyone about it after the fact. If my father were alive, would I have wanted a more traditional wedding and have him walk me down the aisle? I wouldn't change any of it today but what would my father have thought?

I met and married my husband in New York. He immigrated to the United States from Portugal as a young boy. His background is about as far from my Ozarks heritage as one can get. He grew up in two huge, bustling cities of the world, Lisbon and New York City. What would he and my father, the farmer, have in common? Would their diverse worlds get along? I have to go by the opinions of others on this subject. My father loved all kinds of people and learning about them. My husband was born in the city but his heart is in the country. I have no doubt that the two of them would have been great friends. My father could show my husband all the farming tricks and how to get along in the woods. Fishing was a passion for both of them, so they would have had this in common.

Would my father have wanted me to marry someone more local? To this question, I think I have the answer. I don't think he would have cared at all, so long as it was what I wanted. After all, he married my mother who wasn't from the Ozarks. I believe he would have been happy with whomever I chose so long as it made me happy.

Life is full of questions with no answers. These are just a few of mine. Would my life have been any richer or better with my father in it? Of course, it would have been. Would it have ended up any different? To this I will never know. What I do know is that my father has been in my life everyday through my memories and those of others. I see him often. After all, I only have to look in the mirror to see him.

* * * *

PAPA WAS THERE
Ellen Gray Massey, Author

"This is my daughter," my father, Chester H. Gray, would say with great pride as he introduced me to his business associates, to a United States Senator, or to the bellhop at his hotel. He didn't indicate that he had four other daughters and three sons. It was as if I was the one and only. But he wasn't partial just to me. His pride and respect for all eight of us was equal. In an era when boys were more important and had more privileges, he made no distinction.

As a child I thought my father was the smartest man I knew. Now when I'm almost as old as he was when he died, I still think so. To me he was a walking dictionary and encyclopedia.

"Papa, how do you spell Massachusetts?" I would ask while doing my homework on the living room floor. He spelled it out carefully.

"Papa, who was president when Lindbergh flew across the Atlantic?"

Without pausing in his reading of the evening paper he said, "Theodore Roosevelt."

He wasn't upset that I disturbed his reading. He didn't groan or tell me to look up the information. He just added to my knowledge. He was my authority. I never doubted that he knew. Even when I was in high school and college, I took the lazy way out. I asked my father.

In various ways he saw that we were educated up through putting all eight of us through college. He took us on trips, to music performances, world fairs, and anything cultural. School attendance was a given. A two-foot snowfall didn't keep his children home from school. He bundled up the school-age kids and stomped out a path across the neighbor's pasture to the country school. A small ache never was an excuse to stay home. "Going to school is your job," he said. "It is just as important as what your mother and I do."

However, there was one exception to never missing school. When Ringling Brothers, Barnum and Bailey Circus came to town, he came by the elementary school and picked up my younger sister and me to take us to the circus. I think he was sort of sorry when we (the youngest in the family) grew up, as he didn't have anyone to take to the circus.

But his influence didn't stop with formal education. He used other means to teach. He didn't punish us or scold us when we messed up. When I turned sixteen and got my driver's license, I drove my friend in our family car to a movie theater across the city, in an area I wasn't familiar with. When the movie was over late that afternoon and we walked to where we parked the car, it was gone. We hadn't noticed earlier that while parking on the street was permissible when we went into the movie, it was not allowed during later rush hours. Someone told us that the car was towed to a city garage.

Here I was entrusted for the first time with the car and it was towed away. Though I was afraid of what my father would say or do to punish me for my lack of responsibility, I had no alternative but to call him at his office. I was crying into the telephone, but when I heard his voice, like a little child, I knew everything was all right. Papa was there.

"Where are you?" he asked in his normal voice that showed, not anger, but a trace of anxiety. "Just hold on. I'll be there directly."

Fifteen minutes later he was beside me. He took care of everything. When he got behind the wheel and my friend and I piled beside him in the front seat, all he said was, "That was a good experience for you."

My father believed in us. He never doubted that any of us could do whatever we wanted. He started out as a farmer and later became involved in farmers' organizations and worked in Washington, D.C. for many years as the national representative of the American Farm Bureau Federation. Though we moved there, our mother and all the kids still at home came back to our southwest Missouri farm each summer, returning to Washington for the school year.

When I graduated from college, I wanted one last summer to work on the farm. "Can you give me a job?" I asked my father. I was thinking that I would do some field work, like plowing a field for wheat as my brothers did each summer until they graduated and left home.

"You bet," he said. "We need a garage." Then he and I sat in the porch swing while he drew on a slip of paper a plan for a garage. In a half hour of instruction time, he explained the design, the materials I'd need, and the measurements. He wrote out and gave me the order for the lumber and said he'd have a neighbor pour the concrete foundation. Then he went back to

Washington, confident that I could build a garage. I did.

My brothers and sisters and I have talked many times, wondering what he and our mother did to produce a successful family that never fought and has stayed close all our lives, even down to the fifth generation who return to the family farm for regular reunions.

Was it because they had faith in each of us? Or that they behaved toward us in such a manner that, as my oldest brother Harold said, "We didn't misbehave (much) because we did not want to disappoint them?"

Perhaps not wanting to disappoint them was the key. When I was afraid to call my father with the car towing incident, I was crying because I couldn't endure the thought that I might have disappointed my father. Far from that. He treated my failure as part of my education.

✸ ✸ ✸ ✸

MY FATHER'S HUMOR
Carolyn Gray Thornton, Author

If I received an envelope addressed to me in my father's bold handwriting, I knew that it would be a funny poem he wrote in the train as he traveled on his job. The humor he shared was a contrast to the no-nonsense, all-business appearance he presented at other times.

On one April Fool's Day I walked into the bedroom my sister and I shared and found Papa on his back under the bed trying to tie the bed covers to the springs so we couldn't get into bed. I remembered that clearly many years later when he died on April 1st.

I enjoyed seeing him visiting with our rural neighbors, but I also was able to see him talking with senators and representatives in the halls of the Capitol Building in Washington. He was as much at ease with one as the other.

My heritage from my father was a love of the country, family, cats, music and fun, mixed well with a commitment to responsibility and self-assurance. Memories keep these things alive in me today.

****

BORN NEAR HOME
Pauline Manning Batchelder, Genealogist

My father was a sober man (both literally and figuratively), but a loving parent. And he had a sense of humor. I felt very comfortable with him, except when he was being stern.

I can remember, as a little girl, standing behind him and holding onto his trouser leg when I had to meet someone new or when someone asked me a question. I can also remember when he used to throw me into the air over his head and catch me again. I loved that and would laugh. I also remember the last time he did it, after I begged him to. He said,"You're getting too heavy for me to lift that far."

His roots were in the Middle West. William Ray Manning was born December 26, 1871 (the year of the great Chicago fire, he liked to point out), of a family that had homesteaded in Marshall County, Kansas. In 1869 they made a rigorous trip westward, partly by rail (the tracks ended then at the Missouri River), the rest by covered wagon. When they left the train, my grandfather was robbed of all his money.

The Mannings selected a homestead about one and a half miles southeast of Home City. My father was born there--in a sod house, he said. He enjoyed telling people he was born near Home. When the railroad was extended through Marshall County, it went past the southern end of their farm. The family would walk barefoot along the tracks to get to town, carrying their shoes to protect them from damage. The only amenity in the household while he was growing up was a pedal organ which his mother had brought on the journey.

As he grew, my father helped with the farming, but he was smart, did well in school, and wanted to go to college. His mother undoubtedly encouraged him, as she had been a school teacher. Her claim to fame was that Frank James was a pupil of hers in Liberty, Missouri, and one day he brought little brother Jesse to school with him.

By working and saving money he was able to enroll in Baker University, in Baldwin, Kansas. In 1897 a young lady named Mabel Marvel enrolled at Baker, and they soon became interested in each other. One of the college's yearbooks states that Ray was "head over heels." They were married in 1903.

My father's goal had been to become a Methodist minister. But after a couple of years at Baker, his history professor, noting how good he was in his history courses, persuaded him to switch to history. It changed his life. He got a master's degree at the University of Kansas, then enrolled in the history department at the University of Chicago, where he earned his Ph.D. As part of his work he needed to do research in Spain, so he and Mother spent most of their honeymoon there. Working in Seville, in the Archives of the Indies, Daddy found documents pertinent to his subject, and Mother transcribed them by hand. They also did research in Madrid, Paris, and London, then returned home on the ship Carpathia, which later became famous for going to the rescue of passengers on the sinking Titanic.

In the years before I was born, he taught in several universities, but in 1918 he became an official in the Latin American Division of the U.S. Department of State in Washington, D.C. He remained there until his retirement. At times he taught evening classes at American University. He made trips to Cuba, Haiti, and Mexico in connection with his work, and one to a Pan-American Highway Conference in Chile, representing the United States, as the State Department person coordinating the U.S. role in building the Pan American Highway. He later received a decoration from the Ecuadoran government to honor his contribution to the building of the highway.

During many of his years in Washington, my father spent an extra hour every working day on a non-State Department project, publishing several series of books on U.S. relations with the American nations, under the imprint of the Carnegie Endowment for International Peace.

During the State Department years, I entered the family. When I was three, Daddy took me on his lap, opened a Spanish primer (probably bought in Spain) and set to work teaching me to read. I remember the text on the first couple of pages: "Sol sol soldado, soldado sin sol. Sal sal salada, salada sin sal"--with appropriate illustrations. When my first grade teacher found out that I already knew how to read, she seemed a bit cross.

He could also be very strict. I got into a lot of trouble with him one year when I came home from school with three F's on my report card. I know why that happened, but I couldn't explain it to him then. He was furious. He said, "I'm not going to speak to you again until you bring your grades up." He did not relent. I felt terrible; it may have been the worst experience of my childhood. My mother took charge--she tutored me. The next report card had A's on it. My father was pleased, my penance ended, and the matter was never mentioned again.

My father loved gardening--perhaps it was an echo of his farm childhood--and he laid out a small formal garden in the back yard in Washington, surrounding the beds with small boxwoods. In the center he built a fish pond of concrete, and he kept it stocked with goldfish. My friends and I loved to run through the paths in his garden. Several times he won the neighborhood citizens' association's annual competition for best garden.

In those days, the 1920s and 30s, people still made social calls on Sunday afternoons, and it was customary to present a calling card to the person who opened the door. We had an abalone shell in the front hall in which the cards were collected, and it got quite full by the time the custom died out--perhaps with the onset of World War II. I still have those cards stowed away somewhere.

The men would sit in the living room and talk, and the wives would drift off into the kitchen. I always wanted to stay and listen to the male talk--it was much more interesting. The men discussed their work and their colleagues and what was going on in the historian's world.

Daddy liked Dodge cars--never had anything else. The first one I remember was about a 1920 model; it had isinglass windows and was very cold in the winter. We kept a blanket in the back seat for protection.

My father died in 1942, at not quite seventy, of atherosclerosis and finally a heart attack. He needn't have died that soon, but we didn't know much in those days about eating right. Too many chocolate bars, too much cocoa, too much cream? As his health started to fail, his doctor told him to drink a quart of milk a day! There was rarely low fat milk in the stores in those days.

The last event of his life was a happy one, though. He had a reunion with a very old, and close, friend, Dr. Benson Baker, another Kansan, who was a college roommate and went on to become a Methodist minister, spending many years, with his wif as a missionary in India. Their correspondence lasted close to forty years. At the end of that last visit, my father walked out to the bus stop with Ben to see him off, then came back inside, lay down on the couch, as usual, and died.

※ ※ ※ ※

ISN'T THAT WHAT FATHER'S ARE FOR?
Kathryn Mallory Richardson, Missionary

Daddy, you were never "Father" to me...always "daddy" and, to me, that word carries a softness, a caring, a loving connotation. And, your life showed me much of what God, the Father, must be like.

I probably never thanked you for choosing mother as your bride, giving me an exceptional mother and friend.

I probably never thanked you and mother enough for being with me at home when I needed your help and prayers to let Jesus into my heart when I was nine years old and for the years that you took me to church and gave spiritual guidance. After all, isn't that what fathers are for?

I probably never thanked you enough for being a good daddy, being a great example, kind, caring, loving, encouraging: flying kites, catching me when I jumped into the deep end of the swimming pool (I knew I was safe.) After all, isn't that what fathers are for?

I probably never thanked you enough for your generosity. School teachers back in the '30s and '40s didn't make much money. But, thank you for being one of the most generous people I have ever known--with relatives, with friends, with people in need, and especially with my family. After all, isn't that what fathers are for?

I probably never thanked you enough for not complaining or seeking to discourage me as I, along with Bill, took four of your grandsons and moved thousands of miles away. The teardrops fell, but were only accompanied by love. But, after all, isn't that what fathers are for?

I probably never thanked you and mother enough for sharing your home with me and my family during four months of furlough after our first term in Brazil. What patience. But, after all, isn't that what fathers are for?

I probably never thanked you enough for letting our sons know that they had a home with you, a place to go on weekends and holidays when their own home was so far away--a place complete with turkey and ham, sausage gravy, M&Ms, Rook, pocket money, advice, love, trips to cemeteries where family is buried, and to relatives to help them connect, and much, much more.

Now and then, someone says, are you Dillard's (or Ferrell's) daughter, and I proudly say that I am. And often they go on to tell me of the influence you had on their lives. In a cafeteria line one day someone recognized me and told how mother had been her mentor when she was practically bereft of one. Just the other day at a ball game, the man sitting next to me told me how you helped him when he was just a new superintendent still wet behind the ears. Thank you for that heritage. But, after all, isn't that what parents are for?

So, tongue in cheek, I say, "isn't that what parents are for?" Yes, I am sure it is God's plan that all parents should be a blessing to their children. I am sure that is what parents are for. But unfortunately, many never reach that high or attain that goal. And unfortunately, children have little idea of the sacrifices and efforts parents make in their behalf until they are older. And, I thank you for seeing your responsibility, accepting it, and doing it with finesse.

And, just one more thing. When I was thousands of miles away and Arthur Lee called and told me that you were close to being with the Lord, he held the phone to your ear and let me talk to you, thanking you and being able to feel close to you again. I hope you heard.

These and many other blessings are things about which I would like to chat with you. Maybe in eternity we will take a few years to do that. There, I will have much time to thank you and to thank my Heavenly Father for you and for mother and for your love.

* * * *

GIFT OF LIFE AND LEADERSHIP
Arthur Mallory, Educator

Remember the song, "That Silver-Haired Daddy of Mine"? I am not sure that is the correct title and I don't recall the lyrics, but it is a tear jerker. One line goes, "If God would but grant me the power, to turn back the pages of time, I would give all I own, if I could but atone, to that silver-haired Daddy of mine."

I suspect we would all like to do some things over, and many would like the opportunity to say one more thing to those we have loved. I really don't fit perfectly into that category with my Dad. He and I spent a lot of time together during the last years of his life. After he began to require a great deal of help with day-to-day living, I was with him during some part of every day. When he got to the point where his mind worked but he could not express himself verbally, I could finish his sentences for him and pretty well read his thoughts. So, he and I didn't leave much unsaid. He knew of my love for him.

So, if he were available for another conversation, I would wish to again thank him for the really important things he did for our family and me.

I would thank my Dad for living the kind of life I wanted to emulate. I would thank him for being the kindest person I have known. He had a special talent for making a child and young person perform better than he/she had any right to expect. He could make one "play over his head." I would, again, express my appreciation for that. My dad always had more confidence in me than I deserved, but it worked to make me try harder and do more than my ability would indicate possible.

By the time I was a sophomore in high school, I had been given an advanced course in School Administration. My sister Kathryn and I sat at the feet of two master teachers, daddy and mother, and we knew what it took to do a great job in the classroom and office. When I decided to follow my parents in the teaching profession and took my first administrative job, I already had years of experience which came from our parents. I was always grateful for this head start and my Dad knew it. If we could speak with one another again, I would remind him of my gratitude.

Mostly, I would wish to thank my Mom and Dad for leading me to a saving knowledge of Jesus Christ as my Savior. It was no accident that both my sister and I accepted the gift of salvation early. Our parents were purposeful about their duty to teach and model the Christian life. I will never finish being grateful for this gift, and I would again thank Daddy for the role he played in helping secure for me my salvation.

Before Daddy's death, I had the opportunity to tell him of my appreciation for his life and leadership. If I had the opportunity, I would tell him again.

❊ ❊ ❊ ❊

THE BUSINESS OF BEING A FATHER
Robert Mitchell Hale, Businessman

One of my first memories of my father was riding in a pickup truck with my dad, Bob, and my Granddad, Dean. We were checking cows in May of that year. The grass was tall and Dean would reach his arm out the window as we slowly drove through the herd. Grandpa Dean and my dad would pull stems of fescue up and chew on them while grasshoppers bounced off the windshield. And, I even got to chew on the bitter tasting grass. I asked, "How can anything so bad tasting satisfy the cow's hunger?" Dad and Dean explained that a cow has four stomachs and we have one. So, by the time the grass gets to the second stomach it tastes a lot better. This is an example of how everything my dad had me help with was a way of teaching me a lesson. So, while I thought my dad was being hard on me or making me work, I was actually learning life's lessons from him and developing standards for myself such as:

If you work for someone, give them a good days work. Be on time. Your word is your bond. Pay your bills before you take out for yourself.

My Dad was hard for me to communicate with and I never heard him compliment me or say "good job" or "I'm proud of you" or "I love you." But, I would get second hand news from people who told me that my Dad had said how good a salesman I was or the great deal I had put together. So, I knew he was proud of me and that I had become the man he had hoped I would become.

Some days I do things and I think I am morphing into my dad. So, I try to keep the good lessons I learned from him and change the things that were lacking. So, it is easier for me to tell my kids I love them or I'm proud of them.

Dad passed away three years ago and I think of him often. Sometimes, with a smile. Sometimes, with sadness. Sometimes, with anger. I spent the best part of twenty years working as a partner in the same office with him. I think in customer's eyes our work went from me being Bob's son, "the young green kid" to Dad being "Mitch's dad," since twenty years later Mitch was the hub and the voice of experience in our company. I do think through it all my Dad was proud of my accomplishments and was happy for all the times we worked together.

So, Dad, you taught me a lot. Some lessons were trial by fire. Some lessons were results of you putting me in a "sink or swim" situation. Above all, you taught me to be more open with people and not as reserved and sheltered as you were. And, you and my son, Nick, have taught me to say, I love you!

So, even though it's three years too late, I love you, Dad.
Your son and partner, Mitch

* * * *

I could have told my dad I loved him one more time before he passed away.

BUDDIES FOREVER

High in the steeple, the muffled gong, gong, of bells resounded calling the faithful to worship.

Our family walked toward the church. Daddy, handsome in his Sunday suit had slicked down his thick, brown hair for the occasion. Mom, the slender young matron was resplendent in her silk dress. My brother, Rex, was fresh out of short pants, and me, the baby of the family tugged at Daddy's hand as I walked with them.

Daddy lifted me into his arms, and with his eyes crinkling into a smile, he whispered, "Who's Daddy's girl?"

The bells were louder now. Daddy put me down. I reached for his hand, but it slipped away. He walked toward the church.

I called to him, "Don't leave me Daddy. You promised I could sit with you. Remember, I'm your buddy!" Bells, bells, bells.

Daddy turned toward us. He looked at each of us as if memorizing the lines of a favorite poem. He winked at me and pulled the lobe of his right ear. "Buddy's forever."

Automatically, I mimicked Daddy gesture preforming our special ritual as I whispered, "Buddy's forever."

Waving, he disappeared inside the church.

I stomped my foot angrily, demanding, "Why did he leave me, Mama? He didn't even say goodbye."

Shrilling insistently, the bells pierced my dreams. I tried desperately to retain the image of the door through which my daddy had vanished, but it disappeared.

Fumbling in the darkness, I pulled the phone from its cradle before it could wake my husband and children.

"Hello," I whispered.

"Come to the hospital. Your mother needs you and your brother. She says to drive carefully." The faceless voice was gone.

I switched on the bedside lamp.

My husband, Bob, asked, "What's wrong?"

As I repeated the brief message, I searched for an answer, remembering the visit with Dad and Mom at the hospital the evening before.

Pleasure had blushed Dad's cheeks when he announced, "Tomorrow night I'll be sleeping in my own bed."

I leaned over his hospital bed and kissed his bald spot.

Mother smiled. "Tomorrow will be a return to normal for us all."

What had happened?

"You better call Rex," Bob said.

My brother and I puzzled over questions with no answers as he drove the thirty-five miles to the Springfield hospital where Dad had undergone surgery several weeks before.

We rushed through silent, familiar halls. Dad's door was partially closed. Mother hurried with a nurse to intercept us. Too late. The stripped bed glared at us accusingly like a raw wound that would be a long time healing.

Mother confirmed our greatest fears in a prosaic monotone. "I'm sorry, children. Dad's gone."

The nurse tried to usher us from his room but we were drawn to the empty bed. Rex caressed the cold, still bed as if by his touch it might return life.

Short hours before Daddy had promised me, "I'll see you tomorrow."

"You didn't even say goodbye, Buddy," I whispered as my hand reached to caress the lobe of my right ear. Shock numbed my body, isolating it from reality and a growing anger. I was playing my assigned part in a play. But, I was unable to recall my lines.

Strangely calm, mother spoke of the blood clot that had claimed Daddy's life. Rex drew strength from her words.

She looked over his head at me. For the first time, I could see loss in her eyes. She spoke wordlessly, "We must be strong."

The last rituals let us hold Daddy close to us a little while longer. Details claimed us. Family, friends, arrangements for the funeral filled our days.

I took Daddy's hospital clothes home to launder. I savored the familiar smell as I hugged his pajama's wishing it was him. The clothing hung limply mocking me. Angrily, I wadded the material in a ball and tossed it in the washer. Slamming the lid I cried, "Why did you leave me, Daddy. I need you. You're my buddy!"

Bob's arms enfolded me in a hug. "Jane, you got to let go. You're only hurting yourself more. I know."

I returned his hug remembering the recent loss of his father.

The day of Daddy's funeral arrived. Out of town relatives reunited our family with remembrance. The last visit was made to the funeral home before the final service. The clan gathered for dinner.

Suddenly, I was gripped with nostalgia. My Daddy was not in the midst of this family gathering. His laughter would never ring out as the old stories were repeated. I couldn't search out his eyes and share a memory. I would not see Daddy alone again, ever. I started for our car.

Bob caught up with me. "Where are you going?"

"To see Daddy!" I glared at him defensively expecting an argument.

"I'll go with you. Get in." Bob's face held a bereft sadness.

The body lying clothed in its Sunday best was my Daddy, yet fragile, already fading. The sweet smell of floral offerings mingled with an aura of loss.

Oh, Daddy! Silently, I cried for the times he'd miss. He'd not grow old with his wife, children, and grandchildren. Selfishly, I yearned for our special father-daughter relationship, the bond of innocence between a man and woman that was pure, clean, and perfect. He had been my father, my buddy, but more--my playmate, first boyfriend, counselor, financier. He was my shield from the world.

I twisted my hands in anger much as a small girl might

stomp her foot. Looking at the silent face, the closed eyes that would twinkle no more, the busy hands that were stilled in death, I spoke accusingly through my tears, "You didn't even say goodbye."

My husband's arms encircled me. "Your dad never liked tears."

It was true, humor was his forte. I looked one last time at Daddy's face. Then, I kissed his silent lips and whispered, "Goodbye, Daddy. I'll always be your little girl."

We had shared our niche of time together. A thin, scab started to work its way across Daddy's corner of my heart. It would crack open at times, but would heal again because memories are therapeutic.

Our family drove in silence as the long line of cars loaded with kinfolk began the last trip to the funeral services. My sons had been raised in church and knew the promise of eternal life. But they had lived through the loss of one grandfather and knew the final close of the casket lid. Grief etched their faces.

As we emerged from our car, a small hand tucked itself in mine. I looked down into my youngest son's tear-stained face.

"Are we going to see PaPa again?" Mitch asked.

I hugged him to me drawing comfort from him. "We'll see PaPa one last time. Then, we'll have him forever, right here. I patted Mitch's chest over his heart. "Let's go say goodbye to our Buddy."

Daddy's eyes twinkled at me again from my son's face as his tears turned into a smile. He lifted his finger to the lobe of his ear and tugged out the ritual his PaPa had passed on to him. Starting forward, he pulled me with him promising, "Not goodbye, Mom. See you later."

High in the steeple, the muffled gong, gong, of bells resounded calling the faithful to worship.

❊ ❊ ❊ ❊

MEASURING UP TO DAD

A dear friend lost her father a short time ago. She wanted to write a tribute for her father to read at his funeral but doubted her ability to compose it at that time.

These are the words of reassurance I emailed to her. She encouraged me to share these words in *Every Day Is Father's Day.*

"Yes, you can write a tribute for your father's funeral. Do it! Think of your words as the last thing you can do for a man who was more than any man can be in your life. Your father is the one man, with whom you share a pure, clean, relationship. He has the best in his heart for the most precious relationship with a woman that she has with a man, father and daughter. You can do it for the butterfly moments of childhood, the stern moments of teen-years, the giving-up years of young womanhood, and the precious years of being able to share your love by making your father a grandparent and a great grandparent. He gave, you gave, and together, you loved. You can do it for this man, who believed in you.

Stand tall and make him proud. Think not of yourself but of the man who was, is, and will always be, your father. You know you look for him in every man you see, measure every man with whom you seek a relationship by the yardstick of your father. You wonder why those men don't live up to the standards your father set for you. Yes, dear heart, you can do it, in the way that only a daughter, who dearly loved her father, and was more than loved by him, can do. Put those words on paper in the way that only you, as a writer can do. Let them soak into your soul, then share them with the world. Your father will be listening. It can be an intimate, bonding, moment. DO IT! Tears may come but tears are your badge of grief. Remember, your friends love you and will be right there with you, if not in body, in spirit. Our words are the flowers of our writer's relationship. DO IT! And, I expect a copy of your words to use in *Every Day Is Father's Day* with mention of you and your father. So do it with love, but edit it to death as only you can do.

DO IT!

My dad died in the hospital in the sixties. I brought his hospital clothes home with me to wash. I was only thirty something. Gosh, was I ever that young? When I started to put his things in the washer the aroma of him surrounded me. I embraced his discarded clothing and cried. Later, I told Mom. She said she shouldn't have sent the clothing home with me to wash. But, it was more than cleansing of the pajamas that took place that day.

When you lose a loved one as I did, my father, don't hesitate to cry and share your emotions with family. Better to do it while you're together. Later, you'll have tears of your own. However, memories shared with others who loved the deceased sustain you.

These words said, I have yet to cry for my husband, Bob, who died in April of 2003. One day I know it will hit me but for now I keep remembering the day at the funeral home and the funeral my family planned that was so uniquely him. Grief finds us all sooner or later. You just never know what might trigger it.

The Hale Family, left to right: Reggie Dean, Ricky Blaine, Lucas Lee, Bob (standing), Jane, Mitch

Bob died April 27, 2003. A short time, a long time. Time can't be measured by the calendar, only by the heart. He'll always be missed by his family and friends. It's just hard to realize he won't be coming back.

YOU WON'T BE COMING BACK
In memory of Robert Dean Hale (Bob)
Written April 27, 2005.

I turned around
and you were gone.
It's taken me so very long
to realize
you won't be coming back.

I listen close
and hear no sound.
Silence is all I've found,
not you
you won't be coming back.

I step ahead
and look for you
Shaping dreams we two
created together.
You won't be coming back.

I turn around
and find only me
Not two, but one, singly,
shaping tomorrow.
You won't be coming back.

I see our sons
and find you there
recreating love we share.
You're here,
although
You won't be coming back.

Section VI
Rich Man

R ich man, poor man, beggar man, thief
Doctor, lawyer, merchant, chief

Immortality

Peacemaker in The Field of Education

Mr. Basketball

Heroes in Motion

Doctor Tommy

Who can forget the picture of a small boy standing at attention saluting the casket of his father as it passed in front of him while millions mourned the loss of the boy's father, the 35th president of the United States of America, John Fitzgerald Kennedy?

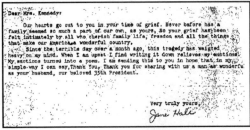

IMMORTALITY

Dallas, Dallas, city of disaster,
when will your tale be told?
Throughout the realm of centuries, this legend will unfold.
A story that every tongue will tell
and every eye will see.
Minds will try but will ne'er will blot
this event in history.

The rain passed over Dallas and the sun
brought crowds to wait.
They asked but a glimpse, a wave, a smile, a
rendezvous with fate.
Amid triumphant cheers they came, heads held
high with trust.
All hail the chief, the President, and then,
the viper thrust.
Insane with hate, it twists and turns and strikes out
at the Nation.
Crushes courage in its wake, then seeks its
own salvation.
The world has stopped and time stands still,
as poison seeks its quest.
Blood, so red, from that noble head soiled pink
a loving breast.

Red roses smashed in turmoil. Then yellow roses, too.
"My God", they cried. "He's shot them both.
Now, what more will he do?"
Shocked with horror, but filled with hope,
on to help they sped.
Only to hear those damning words,
YOUR PRESIDENT IS DEAD.

The kiss of death violently placed its mark
on martyrs brow.
It gave him peace for which he'd begged, replaced him
with a vow.
As the people watched and waited, grief uniting foes
In a bed of bronze they brought him home, lying in repose.

O silent, solemn city, with grief they built his wall.
Mortared with love and heartbreak, stiff with protocol.
A horse without a rider, fatherless children we see.
A country's loss, a family mourns with courageous dignity.

The long, black line lit candles. And the glow reached
far and wide.
Then love gave an eternal flame to live by Courage side.
Thus as she'd loaned him, so she gave him,
shrouded with a flag.
A ring, a kiss, her vigil kept, they gave her back the flag.

O after the crowds have gone, the last taps died away,
The memory commended to history, what more can
the nation say?
Son, Father, President, husband, whoever
remembers the man
Remembers the son who loved the man as only
a son can.

"Ask not what your country can do for you but
what you can do for your country."
John Fitzgerald Kennedy
May 29, 1917 - November 22, 1963

137

Mallory awarding diploma to Reggie Hale, 1971

PACEMAKER IN THE FIELD OF EDUCATION

Some men fashion lives unknowingly. Others realize the reflection of their life in later years. When I attended high school, our superintendent, Dillard A. Mallory, was such a man. As an educator, his influence reached far beyond his family. I think of him as a father of education who shaped many lives, not only in our community, but worldwide.

As I sat in his citizenship class, I learned something he taught every student who came under his tutorship. It stuck with me through the years, and when I meet another student from those years we can easily recite together:

> *He who knows not and knows not that he knows not is a fool.*
> *Shun him.*
> *He who knows not and knows that he knows not is simple.*
> *Teach him.*
> *He who knows and knows not that he knows is asleep.*
> *Wake him.*
> *He who knows and knows that he knows is wise.*
> *Follow him.*

Dillard Mallory was raised in a large family on a small farm in Rural Wright County, Missouri. Times were hard. Cash was scarce. Transportation was slim. By the time young Dillard was ten years old, he had evaluated the world around him and set his sights on one of three careers--mail carrier, preacher, or teacher. These professional people were all highly regarded in the community, they were paid with cash, and they all rode good horses. These things were important to him.

Having a keen mind, he chose the field of education. His decision was justified when he took the county teaching exam after he finished the seventh grade. Dillard made the highest score which granted a first level teaching certificate.

When he was thirteen, Dillard teamed up with an Evangelist for several revivals and spent several summers teaching music schools.

In high school Dillard got his first glimpse of a young lady named Ferrell Claxton who would later become his wife. To help pay for family expenses and the remainder of his high school education, he quit school to teach at the one-room Nation School in Webster County, grades one through eight.

When he started teaching at sixteen, there were 10,000 school districts in the state of Missouri, mostly one-room rural schools. Seventy-two kids in a one-room rural school, ages five to twenty, occupied Dillard's attention during his first year of teaching.

After he graduated from Hartville High School, he continued his education, entering Southwest Missouri State College in Springfield, Missouri. He and Ferrell were married August 10, 1930. Their first home was in Springfield where they attended classes. Dillard delivered papers for the *News and Leader*, fired furnaces, mowed lawns, and washed cars.

In 1934, when their son Arthur was twenty months old, and their daughter Kathryn was one month old, the Mallory family moved to Verona where Dillard had been hired from a field of seventy-five applicants to become the Superintendent of Vernona Schools. He received a contract for nine months at ninety dollars a month. Since rent was five dollars a month and groceries were not as high as today, the family felt pretty well off.

In the spring of 1944, the Buffalo School Board gave him a three year contract as Superintendent of Schools. He reported to work in Buffalo on July 1st. He was a gentleman who dressed in the mode of his profession--business suit, white shirt, tie, polished shoes, and a stylish dapper hat.

His family quickly became a part of the community. Ferrell taught in the school system, Arthur was in the sixth grade, Kathryn in the fifth.

A man of vision, Mallory shared his dream with the community through its schools. Under his leadership, the school board approved programs that made Buffalo Schools the educational pacemaker in the state.

He initiated improvements, personally financing needed classrooms when the district could not afford them and providing housing for staff in order to attract more qualified teachers. In 1952, he qualified the school for AAA state ratings. He encouraged consolation of neighboring smaller schools to enable the district to have better libraries and offer classes in music, art, vocational training, and pre-school. Among other offerings, he developed innovative programs in radio and aviation.

Mallory encouraged sports, employing Eddie Matthews to head the sport programs. In 1949 the boy's basketball team won the last single-class state champion school tournament. From Buffalo, Matthews became head coach at Southwest Missouri State.

Mallory passed on his concern for youth to his teachers and students. Many followed his example. A 1949 graduate, Jack Freeman returned to become his Assistant Superintendent and later Supervisor of Instruction for Missouri State Department of Education. His son Arthur become State Commissioner of Education.

Through the years, D. A. Mallory continued taking classes and teaching courses in education. He taught at SMS and at Drury College where he was granted an honorary doctorate.

He traveled to Russia in the 1960s as an Educational Ambassador. When he returned, he spoke at nine hundred educational and community meetings comparing and sharing the dream of educational growth and the things he had observed on his trip.

Friends, family, and educators from far and wide followed

his lead as he became a pacemaker in education. He died in 1995. The trail of educational firsts he left was unprecedented. His legacy lives on, as it is repeated from generation to generation. Honoring his thirty-two year administration, his portrait hangs in the lobby of the D. A. Mallory Elementary Building on the west campus of the Buffalo Schools. This is a fitting tribute to the man who spent his life helping youth through education.

ન્ટ   ન્ટ   ન્ટ   ન્ટ

MR. BASKETBALL

From a distance the sternness of Coach Eddie Matthew's countenance was misleading. Within handshaking distance, the smile that lurked just beneath the surface waiting to be earned was indicative of his competitive spirit which spurred students to go beyond their realm and athletes to surpass their capabilities. Coffee-shop coaches in southwest Missouri can tell you about the legend who was an all-star coach, a friend and a good man. Tall and thin, Matthews wore the clothes of an athlete with sinewy grace, the tailored suits of a coach with dignified ease, and was known to be a real Christian gentleman.

Home and family cushioned his existence. He was fiercely proud of his wife, Bernice, his son, Edsel, and daughter, Buanna Mae. The comfortable atmosphere surrounding "his family" widened to encompass student bodies, teams, Sunday school classes, and friends who embraced his world.

Bernice said of her husband, "Eddie is a good man. . .so good . . .sometimes I wonder if he is for real. We have a barn behind the house where Eddie milks our cows. Sometimes I slip down there just to see if he ever curses the cows when they kick him. He never does."

Was it always this way for Eddie Matthews, or did he discover the secrets as he grew into the man who was admired and respected by everyone?

Orla Edwin Matthews was born April 23, 1917, in the

community of Fristoe in Polk County, Missouri. He received his high school education at Goodson and Bolivar. While employed as Elementary School Principal in Polk County, he worked his way through college, graduating from Southwest Baptist College in 1937 and Southwest Missouri State in 1947.

Matthews began coaching at Morrisville High School in 1943. Students soon learned his rules were not made to be broken but used as a spring board to championships. Some dropped by the wayside, others excelled. All who followed in his footsteps learned the challenge of sports and the manners of gentlemen and ladies.

Superintendent D. A. Mallory noticed Matthews and his basketball teams at a local tournament, not only for the quality of their game, but for their manner and appearance. The team followed their coach into the gym dressed in sport coats, shirts, and ties. They sat together. They observed together. It showed when they took the court to win.

Eddie Matthews came to Buffalo, Missouri, to teach and coach both boys and girls sports. He quickly became a legend in his own time. The Buffalo boy's basketball team won the last single class State High School Tournament in 1949.

In 1953, Coach Matthews stepped into a "hot spot" when he took over the reins at Southwest Missouri State as head men's basketball coach. Popular coach Bob Vanatta had just led the Bears to two straight national intercollegiate championships at Kansas City.

Matthews proved himself worthy. His legend became stronger as the SMS Bears 1953-54 squad finished third in the national tournament. Among other honors, his team won the MIAA conference championship three times, twice finished second, tied for second twice and was third three times.

Eddie's 'team family' continued to grow as friends of the Bears attached themselves to the Matthew's house hold. His son, Edsel became a star on the team coached by his dad. Buanna Mae attended SMS and was a cheerleader for the Bears.

Eddie Matthews was looking forward, optimistically to the 1964-65 basketball season when in April of 1964 he died of an apparent heart attack. Sports fans and friends throughout the area mourned the loss of the forty-six year old legend who was known as Mr. Basketball.

Dr. Leland E. Traywick, President of SMS said, "Eddie Matthews was admired and respected by all who knew him. The entire student body and faculty of SMS are stunned and shocked beyond all words at the sudden death of our beloved Eddie Matthews. I only hope we can carry on in the great tradition he set."

Coach Eddie Matthews left some large footprints to fill, but the example he set during his lifetime would live on in the lives of those who were touched by his legacy.

❪ ❪ ❪ ❪

HEROES IN MOTION

If only the words existed to aptly describe heroes who champion our dreams. Everyday life is a collector of exhilarating moments needed to lift it from mundane existence to heights of glory. Homage lingers after applause dies away. The world is left with micro-seconds of the mind to create an image of their heroes.

Harry Weber, a self-taught sculptor from Bowling Green, Missouri, doesn't rely on mere words. He uses mental sketches to create physical entities. He molds images of heroes in their own likeness as he works in the metal of bronze to create subjects in three-dimension.

"Each subject creates its own signature in action," said Weber. "I want to capture those micro-seconds of the mind for fans and for people who never saw the champions' moments of glory. You can't pose action. That's why all my sculptures come from sketches."

Weber's work is quickly becoming recognized as bronze, fluid action by people who have viewed his art on display throughout the United States and abroad.

In January of 2000, Weber wanted to sculpt the statue of

legendary golfer Payne Stewart for display in his hometown of Springfield, Missouri, at the Missouri Sports Hall of Fame after his untimely death October 25, 1999. His proposal was accepted by director of the Sports Hall of Fame, Jerald Andrews, and a group from St. Louis, familiar with Weber's large pieces of action portraits of St. Louis Cardinal players.

These men liked his work of baseball stars Stan Musial, Lou Brock, Red Schoendienst, Enos Slaughter, Bob Gibson, Dizzy Dean, and Rogers Hornsby that was garnering attention and wanted the same look for the statue of Stewart. In a unique style, Weber's work captured details of the baseball players, grouped outside Busch Stadium in St. Louis near a life-sized bust of broadcaster, Jack Buck.

Others had seen the artist's thirteen-foot-tall statue of Missouri football coach Don Faurot standing outside the main gate of Faurot Field at the University of Missouri.

His work was being recognized in many ways such as major awards at National Juried Competition, being on the covers of several anthologies, in national magazines, being museum pieces that are a part of permanent collections of the National Dog Museum, The Museum of Fine Arts in Newport, Rhode Island, and in the Baseball Hall of Fame in Cooperstown, New York.

"I like angles and edges. . .things that move and have strength," said Weber. "The trick is to make a portrait that's true to the face, but also true to the moment in time. Fluidity is a goal. I love bronze because it moves really well--it floats out there. It comes alive." With this in mind, Weber began to collect photographs, videos, newspaper clippings, snapshots, newsreels, and magazine pictures of Stewart.

Consultations with the Payne Stewart family and Joe Green, Stewart's close friend aided Weber as he compiled sketches to bridge his free style to three-dimensional art. The result was Payne Stewart's signature golf swing captured in six feet, six inches of fluid motion that was the hero's moment locked in time.

This statue was the beginning of what would become

Legend Walkway at the Missouri Sports Hall of Fame, just south of Springfield.

Outside the two-story building dedicated to sports icons, one can view Harry Weber's bronze busts of legends, Jack Buck, Stan Musial, Bob Broueg, Norm Stewart, Len Dawson, and Don Faurot. October 25th, on the 3rd anniversary of death, a Weber bust of Payne Stewart was unveiled on Legend Walkway at a private family ceremony.

"I pinch myself every morning. As an artist, to be working and producing is what counts. It's a thrill to know that your art is reaching people," said the man who seemed born to sculpt.

Art was no stranger to the Weber family. Harry's father was an architectural engineer. When their son was born in 1942, it came as no surprise to his parents that he was drawing before he could talk. Sketch pads and drawing tools were Harry's favorite toys. His grandfather was a color chemist who exchanged art supplies for sketches and painting of his contemporaries. Great Uncles William and Fred were respected American Impressionists.

Born in the shadow of Busch stadium, Weber dreamed of a baseball career, but in his freshman year at Princeton that chance to become a cardinal was destroyed when the wide swipe of a bat broke every finger on his right hand.

In 1977, he sculpted a series of plaster fox hounds for the Bridlespur Hunt Club. Bronze busts of H. L. Mencken and Walt Whitman were displayed at Union Station along with a fox hunting scene.

While competing in amateur steeple chases and fox hunts, he met his wife, Anne. They were married in 1985 and settled on a 130 acre farm north of St. Louis. She became a constant influence on his work and his best-loved critic.

The artist is quick to point out, "Sculpting is a collaborative effort. I'm grateful I work with guys who know what they're doing." Vlad Zhitomirsky and Mikhail Matveyev of Innovations in Art build the molds. Claude Mette of Fine Arts Limited builds the larger-than-life statues. In the end, he found it all comes down to the foundry. Six months of work relies on thirty second of pouring 2,100 degree heat of molten bronze onto a mold

145

that has to be durable enough to withstand it. At last Harry Weber's work is ready to share with the world for dedications, inductions, and remembered glory.

Then, after the crowds are gone, microphones and cameras tucked away, filmed images and recorded works committed to history for replay, and the deserted grounds lay silent in abandoned disarray, the heroes belong to the world. Crowds, speeches, and accolades are gratifying but sometimes when words fail, silent memories with our heroes is the finest. Thanks to the man, Harry Weber, for making this possible.

DOCTOR TOMMY

Growing up in Marshfield, Missouri, Tommy Macdonnell knew the long hours and low pay a county doctor could expect because his father, C. R. Macdonnell, his maternal grandfather, and uncle, practiced medicine in Webster County. Barter was a method used for paying doctors during depression years. For a home delivery, C. R. received a muzzle-loading rifle, 36-caliber Hawken. Young Tommy hunted squirrels with the gun. In 1955, he won the Webster County Centennial Muzzle Loading Contest. Sharpshooting would prove to be an important episode in his life. C. R., a skilled obstetrician who began his career as Webster County Health Officer in 1928, earned a salary of $25 per month. His duties included visiting all the rural schools, inspecting their water supplies, their outdoor privies, instructing students and teachers in personal health habits, and beginning an immunization program. Years later his son, Tommy, as a physician and legislator, would draft and help pass the statewide comprehensive immunization program

In 1942, Tommy Macdonnell enrolled in Drury College where he enlisted in the army reserves. He studied German and other military disciplines at Southwest Missouri State Teachers College during the summer term.

146

June 1943, he reported for active duty. After basic training in Texas, he was sent to England for specialized training. He became a member of the "Initial Assault Force "O" of the 16th Regimental Combat team of the First Infantry Division-- the first American soldiers to land on the Easy Red Sector of Omaha Beach Normandy France on D-Day June 6, 1944.

An army sharpshooter, he was wounded twice. On the beaches of Normandy during the D-day invasion and at the Battle of the bulge. S/Sgt. Thomas Macdonnell was awarded five campaign bronze battle stars, a silver star metal, and two purple hearts.

"I'm going home to attend medical school," he said. I've done all the killing I'm going to do. I want to start saving lives."

He completed his BS Degree at Missouri University Columbia and his M. D. from Indiana University School of Medicine in 1950. Kansas City General Hospital accepted him for his Family (General) Practice Residence with emphasis in obstetrics and pediatrics 1950-1952.

Macdonnell married Ann Martin, a nurse, in 1952. They moved to Marshfield and started a practice with his father.

"That's when I came by the name, 'Doctor Tommy,'" he said. "One time our receptionist asked a patient, 'Did you come to see Tommy or the doctor?' My father overheard her. He said, 'It's DOCTOR Tommy. He has his M. D. Degree.' From then on he was C. R. and I was Doctor Tommy." Ann Macdonnell was an active partner in the family medical practice. They had eight children.

Dr. Macdonnell practiced obstetrics more than thirty-five years delivering some 4,500 babies, over 2,500 in Webster county. Others were delivered in Springfield where he was an active medical staff member of Burge, Baptist, and St John's hospitals. In 1953 the Macdonnell's built a small clinic near what is now Interstate 44.

Doctor Tommy had drawn up plans when he was a resident at Kansas City General Hospital for the seven bed clinic/hospital with obstetrical, labor and delivery rooms, minor surgery room, fracture room and ambulance entrance which was used extensively for trauma cases occurring along old Highway 66.

Seven of Macdonnell's children attended Southwest Missouri State University. He was able to hand three of them their diploma's as he was a member and President of the Board of Regents for six years, 1979-1981. He was involved in the building of Hammons Student Center and other buildings on campus and instrumental in obtaining $7.5 million approval from Governor Joe Teasdale for a new college library.

Dr. Tommy was active in many community and state affairs. He served as a member of the Board of Directors of Citizen State Banks of Marshfield and Springfield, of Ozark Technical Community College, of the Early Childhood Development Advisory Committee, Springfield Community Task Force Committee, Advocates for a Healthy Community, and Medical director of Webster County Nursing Home district twenty years.

In 1983, Dr. Macdonnell's heart required a quadruple coronary bypass causing him to cut back on his eighteen-hour medical practice day. Combining his experience in the medical field with an interest in the field of government, he waged a successful campaign for State Representative using the campaign slogan "We need a doctor in the House."

At the state capitol in Jefferson City, the Marshfield democrat became an advocate for the health of children, the poor, and elderly. He was appointed chairman of the House Social Services, Medicaid, and the Elderly Committee and Vice Chairman of the House committee on Public Health and Safety.

Former house speaker, Bob Griffin stated, "The money the taxpayers spent on Macdonnell's salary has been returned a thousand fold on the basis of Medicaid and Medicare money he's saved."

The father of eight children and sixteen grandchildren, Dr. Macdonnell's concern for American's youth was evidenced in a bill he backed designed to improve enforcement on selling tobacco products to people under age eighteen by moving the enforcement arm from the Department of Health to the Department of Public Safety.

When going into a restaurant and they ask," Smoking or

non-smoking," think of Dr. Tommy. He required this with his Clean Indoor Air Act.

In 1994, he attempted to retire. Two days later he began working part-time with the State of Missouri Department of Health. In 1995, though he had repeat coronary bypass surgery, he returned to work.

Because of his lifetime of meritorious service, he, on May 28, 1996, was selected to carry the Olympic torch in St. Louis, Missouri.

Doctor Tommy celebrated his 86th birthday January 9, 2006. He and his wife Ann reside on their 245 acre cattle farm west of Marshfield where his phone continues to ring with requests for consultation.

SECTION VII
S houlder High

Angels on My Shoulder

Essence of Man

Dear Readers

Olympic Torch Bearer Dr. Tommy Mac Donnell,
with Escort Jane Shewmaker Hale

ANGELS ON MY SHOULDER

Flanked by an escort, a runner carrying the Olympic torch jogs through streets filled with cheering crowds. This day, this moment, these runners are guardians of the Official Olympic Flame as it makes its way to another Olympic game site. Never, in my wildest dreams did I imagine I would be one of these runners and yet in 1996, I was.

"You can do anything if you believe you can. Set your goal, work toward it. Quitter's never win, winners never quit." Voices float inside my head as my feet move along the gravel road near our family farm where my husband and I have raised four sons.

"Pick'em up. Put 'em down. Girl, you're sixty-one years young. You need to get in shape for the Olympics." Startled, I realize the voice came from my mouth but the words are my dad's. "I know Dad. Believe me. I'm meeting the challenge."

Angels on my shoulder are no surprise to me. Once they were flesh and blood. They were my anchors, my mentors, my role models. One day I turned, and they were gone. Now, they fashion my world. I hear their voices as they consul me. I see their features in my mirror. Their words of wisdom encourage me and give me strength--strength to do the impossible.

My Mom was an Okie who visited Missouri and met my Dad. They courted by letter when she returned home. He proposed, she accepted. He made the trip to Oklahoma where they were married and returned to make their home in Missouri.

Dad's side of the family gathered at his parent's family farm on Sunday afternoons. Summers, Mom would take my brother, Rex, and me to visit her folks in Oklahoma.

Mom's career was homemaker. The children fell under her realm. Since she was a perfectionist, Rex and I were turned out spic and span. We never had a hair out of place, and our skin rivaled the words of the radio ivory soap commercial. Mom rolled my hair into curls and fashioned petite dresses.

She was looking for a lady. "Jane, don't mess your Shirley Temple curls. Nice girls don't wear jeans and hang around the ball park. They never slide into home base."

Mom soon learned she was raising a tomboy. Since the Depression wasn't far behind, she used the jeans Rex outgrew for my play clothes. That suited me fine. A too-big ball cap with Shirley Temple curls pushed beneath fit real good.

Dad encouraged me to follow the tomboy trail. I wished God had made me a boy. It would have been so much easier. "If wishes were horses, beggars would ride, little girl," Dad's voice reminded me.

Rex was older, and a boy, so Mom made me his charge. Because Mom let the burden of my responsibility rest on Rex's shoulders, it gave me the advantage of learning sports in a boy's world.

I trailed Rex to make-shift ball diamonds where rag-tag kids played sandlot baseball. "Hey, you guys," Rex said, "If you're short a player my sister can play outfield. It'll give her something to do and keep her out of trouble." So, instead of watching from the sidelines, I made use of a batter's glove and chased flies in the outfield. Chasing balls made me a fast runner.

I soon grew tired of chasing balls and began catching them and throwing to the bases. When Rex began to play organized sports, I was his practice catcher. Hanging around the bullpen, I absorbed the wisdom of coaches who preached, "Think you can and you can. . . no play is impossible if you push yourself to the limit. . .on any given night any team is capable of winning" and "practice makes perfect." I never heard the phrase, "It's not whether you win or lose, it's how you play the game" until I was grown. In our sport circles, WINNING was everything. Losing was for wimps!

I can see Rex, stretched out near the radio, ball cap covering his face. (Mom's brother, Uncle Don, gave Rex that ball cap. He wore it to bed until Mom made him quit.)

"The wind up. The pitch. A low, outside curve. Musial swings. . . and, it's going . . .going . . .it's gone! St. Louis Cardinal, Stan Musial, won seven National League batting titles. He became the eighth player to make more than 3,000 hits in the major leagues in the forty's and fifty's." Rex could quote stats like that all day.

My hometown was small, but it boasted a ball diamond where semi-pro baseball teams played. That diamond was a special place for Rex and his friends. It became our second home. At one time, Mickey Owens played on that field with our town's semi-pro baseball team. That was after Owens made a name for himself in the Major League with the Brooklyn Dodgers and jumped down to play in Mexico, along with several other Major League Players. Mom sewed Rex a shirt from good, heavy, muslin. I carried it with me collecting our friend's autographs. Mom embroidered the signatures. Mickey Owen's name is printed boldly on the back yoke. Many hours went into the making of that shirt. Many of those who signed it are still around. Many of them are gone. Memories on muslin. As long as someone takes care of the shirt, it'll be around, just like the game of baseball and all who love the game.

My grandpa on Mom's side was a wiry little Oklahoma gentleman from Tennessee. He wore work clothes with a dapper air. His cheeks harbored snuff and he could hit a spittoon a mile away. Bingo!

His grandkids could listen to his stories all day. "You think fighting proves you're a man. I think fighting's a last resort. Now, running, there's a sport. If it comes to a choice between fighting and running, I'd chose running any day. I'd rather hear them say, "There he goes than there he lays."

The memory of Oklahoma summers linger. Complete, carefree family camaraderie was lounging lizard style, bone lazy in the afternoon liquid sunshine. We'd defrost our minds to listening level by sucking on the frosty mouth of an icy bottle of cola spiked with peanuts, as we became gospels of Grandpa. We swallowed his words, whole, like chunks of icy, dislodged pop. They became a part of our minds, bodies, and souls. And, then we chose to play baseball, his favorite sport.

In high school, volleyball was a new game to me. . .a game for tall girls, if you wanted to spike. I did. We were fortunate to have Eddie Matthews as our coach.

"You're pushing five foot, six inches, kid. If you're going to spike, practice jumping. When you can jump high enough to reach your fingers over the net, come and talk to me. Until then you're a sitter," Coach Matthew counseled.

I stretched, jumped, and one day showed Coach Matthews how I could reach my fingers over the net. Then, he challenged me to strengthen my fingers for the downward placement of a spike. Coach Matthews gave you incentive. He made you reach for your goal. When you reached that goal, he encouraged you to set a higher one.

The lessons learned as a child surface when Angels sit on your shoulder. Dad's father being a farmer used different illustrations. "Life's like an empty basket. Dreams are like apples you pick to fill the basket. Like apples, some dreams are good, others are rotten. It's up to you to pick the good ones. Your basket will be as full as you make it."

"Grandpa, how will you know if a dream is rotten?"

"Did you ever bite into a rotten apple, girl?"

"Yeah."

"What did you do?"

"I spit it out and threw the apple away, especially when I saw a worm in it."

"You get the picture, girl."

Memories of those childhood days are vivid Norman Rockwell paintings in my mind. . .priceless. Their value increases with age as does the wisdom derived from them as I listen to Angels on my shoulder.

Mom's goal was writing. She wrote poems, letters, and stories. Her love of writing was passed on to me as was our family's love of sports. As one grows older, active participation in sports gives way to bleacher support. The dream is passed along to another generation while reaching for more attainable goals. Fingers that once gripped a ball now curve to fit the keyboard of a computer and turn those dreams into freelance articles and books.

An interview of a dear friend Dr. T. M. Macdonnell was in progress when I discovered his profile fit perfectly with the opportunity to nominate him to become a torch bearer for the 1996 Olympics. I nominated him. He was accepted, and I became his escort. We received word we would be carrying the torch in St. Louis, Missouri on May 28th.

I've almost reached the end of my morning run as I prepare for the Olympics. Who'd ever thought a small town girl growing up in the mid-west in the thirties would be preparing for the 1996 Olympics? Dad did. Mom did. Brother did. Grandma did. Grandpa did. Coach did . . . and they consul me as I ran each morning striving to reach my goal. "Don't embarrass yourself, girl. Be ready. Exercise those latent muscles. You come from good stock. We're proud of you! Live your dreams."

"I hear you, all of you! Stay with me while I run. I'm listening. With your help, I know we'll make it for our part in the Olympics."

During the ancient Olympic Games, a holy torch burned continuously on the altar of Zeus. The Olympic flame once again blazed in Olympia, Greece. Over the weekend, a parabolic mirror focused the heat of the sun on an ancient bowl filled with olive leaves and branches, setting them ablaze and the long journey began.

May 28, 1996, flanked by escort Jane Shewmaker Hale, Olympic Torch bearer Dr. T. M. Macdonnell jogged through the streets of St. Louis, Missouri, filled with cheering crowds. This day, this moment, these runners are guardians of the Official Olympic Flame as it makes its way to another Olympic game site. Hereafter, they will be a part of that flame which will always travel to the place where sports is King and dreams come true, if you believe.

ESSENCE OF MAN

While browsing the pages of this book,
I hope you enjoyed the trip you took.
Aftershave, smoke, essence of leather,
Sports section, news, expert on the weather.
Angel on your shoulder
Or the devil to pay
Yesterday, tomorrow, and today
Every Day Is Father's Day.

Dear Readers,

I know you all have memories like mine, think about it. Our life is a roadmap of places, people, and things that junction memory. Some are cul-de-sacs, others criss-cross throughout our days on earth and continue charting journeys for those who follow in our footsteps.

Every Day Is Fathers Day brings together segments of my life and those lives I've touched as I traveled the hills, valleys, and super-highways.

No, my friends and family are not all here but O, the ones that are make for an excellent journey.

Being raised with a brother and having raised four sons and a husband I can vouch for the closing words of this book getting a chuckle from most men.

"Food is one of our greatest enemies, especially as we grow older," a noted physician said while speaking to a group of senior citizens.

"Soft drinks eat our stomach lining. Foods high in fat can kill you. Red meat is bad for your system. However, there's something that is the most dangerous thing of all to eat. We have probably all eaten it or will at sometime in our life. Can anyone tell me what food causes the highest degree of heartache and pain?"

A stout gentleman stood, patted his lady's shoulder, grinned, and said, "Wedding cake?"

NATIONAL CENTER FOR FATHERING

"My dad means to me love…someone to teach me…someone to make sure that I am okay in every way, someone to be proud of and someone to make proud of me."

Every child needs a dad that they can count on. Children thrive when they have an involved father—someone who loves them, knows them, guides them, and helps them achieve their destiny. At the National Center for Fathering we inspire and equip men to be the involved fathers, grandfathers, and father figures their children need. We can be reached online at **www. fathers.com**, via email at **dads@fathers.com** or toll free at 800.593.DADS.

The National Center for Fathering was founded in 1990 by Dr. Ken Canfield in response to the dramatic trend towards fatherlessness in America. Providing research-based training and practical resources, NCF reaches more than one million dads annually through seminars, small group training, weekly email, daily radio programming and our award-winning website, **www.fathers.com**.